ML Sto

D0845491

297
T734i
Tritton, Arthur Stanley
Islam

DO NOT REMOVE
CARDS FROM POCKET

ALLEN COUNTY PUBLIC LIBRARY

FORT WAYNE, INDIANA 46802

You may return this book to any agency, branch,
or bookmobile of the Allen County Public Library

DEMCO

Islam

This is a volume in the Books for Libraries collection

ISLAM

See last pages of this volume for a complete list of titles.

ISLAM

Belief and Practices

A.S. Tritton

BOOKS FOR LIBRARIES
A Division of Arno Press
New York 1980

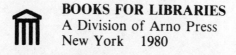

ALLEN COUNTY PUBLIC LIBRARY
FORT WAYNE, INDIANA

Publisher's Note: This book has been reproduced from the best available copy.

Editorial Supervision: Steve Bedney

Reprint Edition 1980 by Books for Libraries, a Division of Arno Press Inc.

Copyright © 1951 by Hutchinson's University Library

Reprinted by permission of the Hutchinson Publishing Group, Ltd.

ISLAM
ISBN for complete set: 8369-9259-8
See last pages of this volume for titles.

Manufactured in the United States of America

Library of Congress Cataloging in Publication Data

Tritton, Arthur Stanley, 1881-1973.
Islam.

(Islam)
Reprint of the ed. published by Hutchinson's University Library, London, New York, in series: Hutchinson's university library: world religions.
Bibliography: p.
Includes index.
1. Islam. I. Title. II. Series: Islam (New York)
[BP161.T68 1980] 297 79-52566
ISBN 0-8369-9269-5

ISLAM

2185797

HUTCHINSON'S UNIVERSITY LIBRARY

WORLD RELIGIONS

EDITOR:

THE REV. PROFESSOR E. O. JAMES

M.A., D.LITT., PH.D., D.D., F.S.A.

Professor of the History and Philosophy of Religion in the University of London

BY THE SAME AUTHOR

Rise of the Imams of Sanaa

Caliphs and their Non-Muslim Subjects

Teach Yourself Arabic

Muslim Theology

ISLAM

BELIEF AND PRACTICES

by

A. S. TRITTON

M.A., D.LITT.

Late Professor of Arabic at the School of Oriental and African Studies, University of London

1951

HUTCHINSON'S UNIVERSITY LIBRARY

Hutchinson House, London, W.1

New York *Melbourne* *Sydney* *Cape Town*

Printed in Great Britain by
William Brendon and Son, Ltd.
The Mayflower Press (late of Plymouth)
at Bushey Mill Lane
Watford, Herts.

CONTENTS

PREFACE

A SHORT account of the essentials of Islam can be adequate but a full account of all local variations would take volumes; here only some of the typical and more striking variants are given. All dates are given in the Christian era; the Muslim began in A.D. 621. Names of persons from the Bible are in the form familiar to the English. Most passages from the Koran are taken from Rodwell's version. The phrase 'Muḥammad said' is used instead of the more correct 'Muḥammad is reported to have said'; constant repetition is boring. Muslims do not like to be called Mohammedans because this name suggests that they worship their prophet.

CHAPTER I

MUḤAMMAD AND THE KORAN

A TRADE road as old as history ran along the west side of Arabia not far from the coast; it survived the discovery of the sea route to India. Near the middle of the road the town of Mecca lay in a barren valley; it was a sanctuary and near by were others which were the scene of annual fairs. Nowadays Mecca lives on the pilgrimage, in the Middle Ages it was dependent on gifts of supplies from Egypt, and earlier it can only have survived by its holiness and its trade. The chief holy place in Mecca was the Ka'ba, a building twelve yards by ten and fifteen high, suggestive of the simplest house. In one corner of it was the Black Stone. It is said that the tribe of Quraish were bedouin in the neighbourhood till they made themselves masters of the town shortly before 500. A hundred years later they were townsmen and traders.

Little is known of the religion of Arabia; names of gods and goddesses are preserved but little more. It seems that they had some idea of a supreme God (Allāh) but he was eclipsed for working purposes by the local or tribal god. Yemen had its own religious system different from that of the north and centre. Some of the northern tribes were Christian even if, as a Muslim said, their Christianity consisted in drinking wine. Jews were strong in the south and were to be found in many places along the west side of the peninsula.

Some were not satisfied with the current religion; one became a Christian, another abstained from idol worship, from flesh which had been offered to idols, from eating blood, from drinking wine, and some wore sackcloth. About the year 600 several men and one woman came forward as religious leaders; some were doubtless urged on by the success of Muḥammad; one, who was given by his enemies the contemptuous diminutive name, Musailima, little Muslim, may have been a genuine enthusiast but we cannot be sure because all we know about him comes from prejudiced sources.

In this world Muḥammad came forward as a preacher of judgement. He belonged to one of the minor families of Quraish; this probably means that he grew up familiar with the shady side of life in a holy city which was probably as bad as other holy places. However the call came to him, he was impelled to preach the terrors of the last judgement with the rewards and penalties of the future life. With this was combined emphasis on the supremacy of the one God, the creator. Reverence for the Lord of the worlds soon grew into an attack on all who had usurped His power, the local deities of the Arabs. At this stage in his teaching, the whole duty of man lay in believing God's message and helping the poor and weak. Frequent prayers, especially at night, honesty in business are commended, and the burying alive of girl babies is condemned.

Some early passages show the style of the preacher and his insistence on a few ideas; the strange oaths are characteristic of the first period of his mission.

By the star-bespangled heaven!
By the promised day!
By the witness and the witnessed!
Cursed the masters of the trench
Of the fuel-fed fire,
When they sat around it
Witnesses of what they inflicted on the believers!

Woe to every backbiter, defamer!
Who amasseth wealth and storeth it against the future!
He thinketh surely that his wealth shall be with him for ever.
Nay! for verily he shall be flung into the crushing fire;
And who shall teach thee what the crushing fire is?
It is God's kindled fire,
Which shall mount above the hearts *of the damned*;
It shall verily rise over them like a vault,
On outstretched columns.

What thinkest thou of him who treateth our religion as a lie?
He it is who thrusteth away the orphan,
And stirreth not *others* up to feed the poor.
Woe to those who pray,
But in their prayer are careless;
Who make a show of devotion,
But refuse help to the needy.

The blow! What is the blow?
Who shall teach thee what the blow is?
The day when men shall be like scattered moths,
And the mountains shall be like flocks of carded wool,
Then as to him whose balances are heavy—his shall be a life that shall please him well:
And as to him whose balances are light—his dwelling-place shall be the pit.
And who shall teach thee what the pit is?
A raging fire!

When the earth with her quaking shall quake
And the earth shall cast forth her burdens,
And men shall say, What aileth her?
On that day shall she tell out her tidings,
Because thy Lord shall have inspired her.
On that day shall men come forward in throngs to behold their works,
And whosoever shall have wrought an atom's weight of good shall behold it,
And whosoever shall have wrought an atom's weight of evil shall behold it.

When the heaven shall cleave asunder,
And when the stars shall disperse,
And when the seas shall be commingled,
And when the graves shall be turned upside down,
Each soul shall recognize its earliest and latest actions.
O man! What has misled thee against thy generous Lord,
Who hath created thee and moulded thee and shaped thee aright?

In the form which pleased Him hath he fashioned thee.
Even so; but ye treat the judgement as a lie.
Yet truly there are guardians over you—
Illustrious recorders—
Cognizant of your actions.
Surely amid delights shall the righteous *dwell*,
But verily the impure in hell fire;
They shall be burned at it on the day of doom,
And they shall not be able to hide themselves from it.
Who shall teach thee what the day of doom is?
Once more. Who shall teach thee what the day of doom is?
It is a day when one soul shall be powerless for another soul: all sovereignty on that day shall be with God.

It needs not that I swear by the stars of retrograde motions
Which move swiftly and hide themselves away,
And by the night when it cometh darkening on,
And by the dawn when it brighteneth,
That this is the word of an illustrious messenger,
Endued with power, having influence with the Lord of the throne,
Obeyed there by *angels*, faithful to his trust,
And your compatriot is not one possessed by jinn;
For he saw him in the clear horizon:
Nor doth he grapple with heaven's secrets,
Nor doth he teach the doctrine of a cursed Satan.
Whither then are you going?
Verily, this is no other than a warning to all creatures;
To him among you who willeth to walk in a straight path:
But will it ye shall not, unless as God willeth it, the Lord of the worlds.

This preaching made little progress among the business men of Mecca. To drive his message home Muḥammad told stories of prophets of olden times; these all saw their message rejected and disaster fell on those who had refused to listen. Mecca was not impressed. In 621 he accepted an invitation to Medina whose inhabitants hoped that his influence would enable the warring clans to live together in peace. In Mecca Muḥammad had tried to create a religious frame of mind in his adherents; in Medina a new religion was born. Muḥammad was now the head of a state, small and divided against itself; in it were the emigrants from Mecca, the Medina clans of Aws and Khazraj which had not had time to forget the 'blood between them', and Jews. Between these factions he had to walk carefully but he had one great advantage, he knew what he wanted and had a policy. His adversaries had none. He had hoped to win over the Jews; when this hope failed, the direction of prayer was changed from Jerusalem to Mecca and the Jews in Medina were banished or exterminated. He now began to call himself a prophet and claimed that he was only repeating the message which God had given to Abraham. Apparently he had learnt that Abraham was the ancestor of both Moses and Jesus and thought to prove his superiority by attaching himself to the source of both religions, Judaism and Christianity. He called Abraham a *ḥanīf*, the name given to those Arabs who had disowned idolatry. The idea of revelation was static; what had been made known to Abraham had been revealed again to Muḥammad. The laws of the Jews were explained away as having been imposed on them for their sins; indeed, one story says that Jacob imposed the restrictions on himself when he was ill. Both Jews and Christians had corrupted their scriptures, especially by eliminating the references to Muḥammad. He was less bitter towards Christians because he had not come into contact with a Christian state; he spoke well of monks though he condemned what he thought were the specific doctrines of the faith.

The Muslim state was born along with the religion in this last period of Muḥammad's life; he was at once prophet and ruler so Islam cannot be divided into church and state. The infant state grew up in the midst of strife so war for the sake of God and religion was a duty. God's command is, "Fight for the cause of God", "Be not fainthearted then; and invite not the infidels to peace when ye have the upper hand: for God is with you". According to tradition Muḥammad was called in the Jewish scripture, 'prophet of strife and war'; he himself is made to say, "I was sent with the sword; what is good is with the sword and in the sword". Laws were laid down and previous customs ruled unless they conflicted with Islam. Muḥammad's character degenerated somewhat through the possession of power but a religious spirit still pervades the later parts of the Koran.

> There is no piety in turning your faces toward the east or the west, but he is pious who believes in God, and the last day, and the angels, and the Scriptures, and the prophets; who for the love of God disburses his wealth to his kindred, and to the orphans, and the needy, and the wayfarer, and those who ask, and for ransoming, who observes prayer, and pays the legal alms, and who is of those who are faithful to their engagements when they have engaged in them, and patient under ills and hardships, and in time of trouble; these are they who are just, and these are they who fear the Lord.

Muḥammad said, "A prayer in this mosque (Medina) is worth more than thousands performed in others, except that in Mecca; that performed there is worth one hundred thousand more than that performed in others. Worth more than all this is the prayer which some one says in his house, where no one sees him but God and which has no other object than to draw near to God." "Avoid what is forbidden, then you will be the most zealous in the service of God; be content with what God has given you, you will be the richest; do good to your neighbour, you will be a believer; wish for men what you wish for yourself, you will be a Muslim; laugh not overmuch, for much laughter kills the mind."

In this connection it is to be noted that before doing any religious act a Muslim must form the intention to do it. Of course this often degenerates into formalism but as often it prevents the parrot-wise repetition of words and actions.

God is separate from the world He has made for "nothing is like Him" yet Muḥammad is never tired of using the wonders of creation and birth to prove that He is and does not abandon those who trust in Him. He has all power so man must bow before Him in humility and accept what He sends. Hence the name Islam, an infinitive meaning 'surrender' and Muslim, the active participle from the same root. Yet at other times man is exhorted to be up and doing. Many texts in the Koran say that God moves man as He wills and as many more assert that man is his own master. The acceptance of Islam blots out a man's past; he starts life afresh and any sins he may have committed are no more reckoned against him.

The method of revelation is imagined as mechanical; the divine message was brought by the archangel Gabriel, who is called the holy spirit, to the prophet who repeated what he had heard. To anticipate a little, the orthodox belief is that every word in the Koran was dictated by God, written by the 'pen' on the 'preserved tablet' and revealed to Muḥammad as circumstances demanded. The earliest communications were in rhymed prose, it might be called free verse, though that would scandalize believers. There can be little doubt that this was in imitation of the pagan soothsayers and diviners for the Arabs had learnt to expect messages from the unseen to have this form.

The Koran contains the revelations given to Muḥammad. These had not been collected during his lifetime though partial collections had been made. A definitive collection was begun during the reign of his successor and this was revised during the reign of 'Uthmān; there is no reason to doubt the authenticity of the result. Sooner or later all texts, which varied from this standard, were suppressed. It must be remembered that the imperfect script of the time was more like a shorthand report of a speech than the printed version. The methods of collection varied; short prosaic pieces were often joined together to make long chapters; many of the short poetical passages were left as separate chapters. Finally the resultant chapters were arranged roughly in accordance with length, beginning with the longest. The Shī'a admit two chapters which are not in the customary text but they combine chapters 93 and 94 into one and also 105 and 106 so that the total remains one hundred and fourteen. The contents fall into two groups, those delivered at Mecca and Medina respectively. In the first, allusions to current events are few, and as little is known about Muḥammad's life at Mecca there are no external means of dating the various pieces, the only grounds for deciding their order are stylistic. The earliest show a vigorous imagination and considerable mastery of language and sound while the moral and religious enthusiasm cannot be mistaken. In the Medina period are references to current events and the history is well known so the sections can be dated. The sentences are long and unwieldy so that the hearer has to listen carefully or he will miss the rhyme altogether; the language has become prose with rhyming words at intervals. The subject matter is laws, comments on public events, statements of policy, rebukes to those who did not see eye to eye with the prophet, Jews especially, and references to his domestic troubles. Here imagination is weak and stock phrases are dragged in to conceal the poverty of ideas though occasionally the earlier enthusiasm bursts out. Muḥammad's conviction that he was the agent of God is responsible for the command to 'obey God and His apostle' but constant combination of the two names leads to such expressions as 'be content with what God and His apostle have given you', which is really blasphemy, while epithets like 'merciful', which are usually reserved for God, are given to Muḥammad. Passages, which belong towards the end of the time in Mecca, descend gradually to the flatness of the latest revelations. There are stories with a moral and these are as dull as such stories usually are and the same ideas are repeated again and again, giving ground for the suggestion that Muḥammad was not satisfied with the literary form of these stories, so that his rough drafts have been preserved along with the final text. Some bits read more like notes for a speech than the finished article. One group of these revelations is marked by the use of the name Raḥmān (merciful) for God; this name was used in south Arabia and it looks as if Muḥammad had tried to make it popular with his followers, had failed and therefore dropped it.

It must not be forgotten that the Koran was made to be heard and the Arabs delight in what sounds to us a jingle.

Literature has preserved a few verses which are said to have been part of the Koran. One is, "If a son of Adam had two rivers of gold, he would covet yet a third, and if he had three, he would covet yet a fourth unto them; neither shall the belly of a son of Adam be filled, but with dust. God will turn unto him who shall repent."

It must never be forgotten that Muḥammad was a preacher. In Medina Islam became a state and a state brings in politics. Consequently the phrase 'God and His apostle' becomes frequent; obedience to the head of the state is obedience to God. The state must be defended, by force if need be. The vocabulary of politics is applied to God and the result jars on our sense of what is fitting, however the words may be translated; 'men plot against God but He is the best of plotters', or, 'play tricks on God but He is the best of tricksters'. It is wrong to be led away by words; this is only the preacher's way of saying that God is the absolute Ruler and all the craft and force of politicians will fail before His ordinances. Believers must do their best to extend the sway of Islam which is the rule of God and their efforts will have His all-powerful backing. It is too much to say that Muḥammad expected Islam to become a world religion but probably he expected it to extend beyond Arabia. Taken literally what he says about false gods is inconsistent; again and again he says that they are nothing, yet they will be summoned at the judgement to condemn those who claimed to have been led astray by them. 'Loving' is applied to God twice in the Koran but the meaning to be read into the word is indicated by such phrases as "God loves those who do good" and "God does not love evil doers". A standard commentary explains love as "the will to do good to someone". The love of man for God is mentioned but it is interpreted as 'veneration'. Orthodoxy with its insistence on the transcendence of God cannot use the idea of love; that was left to the mystics.

In six passages of the Koran there is a hint of an intermediary between God and man. Three quotations are enough:

> The spirit is from the *amr* of its Lord. (17, 85).
> He reveals in every heaven its *amr*. (41, ii).
> He controls the *amr* from heaven to earth and it ascends to Him again (32, iv).

None of the accepted meanings of *amr* fit all the passages so it is suggested that here is something like the '*memra*', the word of God, of Jewish theology (*memra* is from the same root as *amr*) which denotes a personified agency bridging the gap between the transcendent God and the world of change and growth.

There is constant communication between the upper and lower worlds; magic is one form of it. The revelations given to pagans are real but are falsified by the mediums, spirits or men, who distort them. The unbelievers asked Muḥammad for a sign to prove his mission but he asserted that the Koran was a sufficient sign. 'Sign' became the name for a single verse of the book. Muḥammad insisted that he was only a man and had no supernatural power; he was only the mouthpiece of God.

There are seven or ten different 'readings' of the Koran; these are for the most part what the English word implies, different ways of pronouncing the text, elision or assimilation of certain letters. Many variants in the vocalization are recorded but they are so slight as to be negligible, except for specialists; they make no vital difference to the sense. One old mistake seems to have been perpetuated. A word which normally means 'despair' must mean 'know'; some try to get this meaning by hermeneutic methods, others say that in one dialect of the language this word does mean 'know'. It is more natural to suppose that the Kufi or early cursive script with no diacritical points was misread and no one dared to correct the mistake. Similar mistakes are recorded later.

The contents of the Koran were early divided into the obvious and the ambiguous, "some of its signs are of themselves perspicuous—these are the basis of the Book—and others are figurative. But they whose hearts are given to err, follow its figures, craving discord, craving an interpretation; yet none knoweth its interpretation but God". It was recognized that some passages were capable of more than one interpretation; these were to be explained in the light of those whose meaning was beyond doubt.

Also some verses had been cancelled by later revelations, "whatever verses we cancel, or cause thee to forget, we bring a better or its like". To give one example, the verse, "Verily, those who believe (Muslims), and they who follow the Jewish religion, and the Christians, and the Ṣābians—whoever of these believeth in God and the last day, and doeth that which is right, shall have their reward with their Lord; fear shall not come upon them, neither shall they be grieved," is cancelled by, "Whoso desireth any other religion than Islam, that religion shall never be accepted from him, and in the next world he shall be among the lost". Another example is, "Many of the people of the Book desire to bring you back to unbelief after ye have believed, out of selfish envy, even after the truth has been clearly shown them. But forgive them". It is cancelled by, "Make war upon such of those to whom the Book has been given as believe not in God, or in the last day, and who forbid not that which God and His apostle have forbidden, and who profess not the profession of the truth, until they pay tribute out of hand, and be humbled", and also by, "When the sacred months are passed, kill those who join other gods with God wherever ye shall find them, and seize them, besiege them, and lay wait for them with every kind of ambush; but if they shall convert, and observe prayer, and pay the obligatory alms, then let them go their way". Some modern Muslims try to prove that this cancellation is never contradiction but only limitation. This must be called casuistry.

For liturgical purposes the Koran is divided into thirty equal parts. Merit is to be got by reading the Koran so thirty readers would be attached to the tomb of a great man, each of whom would read one part every day. Another division was into sixty parts. At the beginning of twenty-nine chapters stand detached letters, either singly or in groups. Nobody knows what they mean; suggestions made by European scholars are as wild as those made by the Muslims; an eastern Christian saw in the groups of three letters an indication of the Trinity! For only one of these letters has a plausible explanation been offered. The letter N stands at the head of a chapter about Jonah who is known as the 'man of the fish'; N is the initial of *nūn* which means 'fish'. It is perhaps worth notice that Jonah is the only writing prophet of the Old Testament to be mentioned in the Koran.

Muḥammad had to find new words to express ideas unfamiliar to his hearers; broadly speaking, he adapted Arabic verbs and borrowed nouns from other tongues. For 'reveal' he used 'send down' and the root *w-ḥ-y* which may mean, 'point out, write, speak softly'. The names for public worship *ṣalāt* (it is usually translated by prayer) and for the legal alms *ẓakāt* are Aramaic while Jehannum comes from Hebrew, possibly by way of Ethiopic.

The religion which Muḥammad preached was eclectic but that does not hinder it from being a real religion. His debt to the Bible is obvious to anyone who has eyes to see; it may be that his religious life was started by suggestions received from outside the Arab circle of ideas. He took stories from both Testaments to illustrate and enforce his ideas about God, providence and the last judgement. Man being what he is no one can invent a new religion entirely unlike those which have gone before. The Koran often mentions prayers at night; they cannot be separated from the nocturnal services of the monasteries. One cannot escape the impression that Muḥammad purposely made the observances of his religion different. The five daily prayers were in antithesis to the hours of the church. The fast was at first copied from the Jews but was later changed to something more like the Christian practice, again with a difference. Christians used the *nāqūs* to announce the time of public worship and the Jews used the ram's horn on the day of atonement and the new year; the Muslims employed the human voice. Muḥammad chose Friday as the day for public worship—again the difference—but he did not make it a day of rest, perhaps borrowing the idea from Zoroastrianism from which was taken also the bridge across hell along which all must pass. The pilgrimage came from pagan Arabia. It was maintained as part of the policy by which the inhabitants of Mecca were reconciled to Islam. After the conquest the new converts there received many gifts from Muḥammad to the disgust of the people of Medina, both Helpers and Emigrants, who felt themselves slighted and wronged. Muḥammad had to defend himself and did so on the ground that he was binding the hearts of the new Muslims more tightly to Islam. It is hard to resist the conclusion that the retention of the pilgrimage was to preserve the profits of it to Mecca and make it worth the citizens' while to be Muslims. At the same time it was adapted to the religion of Abraham. He and Ishmael had built the Ka'ba, the course between Ṣafā and Marwā was in memory of Hagar's frantic search for water for her son, and the well Zemzem was the source which was given to her by a miracle.

At the death of Muḥammad most of Arabia was nominally Muslim. The 'apostasy' that followed his death was a revolt against the supremacy of Medina though historians looked at it through religious spectacles and interpreted it in terms of faith. Once Arabia was reduced to obedience and the armies marched beyond its frontiers, Islam ceased for a time to be a proselytizing religion. The picture of the Muslim soldiers advancing with a sword in one hand and a Koran in the other is quite false. Not till seventy years after the death of Muḥammad did a caliph arise who was more interested in converting his subjects than in taxing them.

Muḥammad disclaimed any power of working miracles and, when asked for a sign, pointed to the Koran, asserting that men had tried to imitate it but had failed. One man said that there was nothing miraculous in the Koran itself, the miracle was that men had been prevented from imitating it. The supreme excellence has become the official doctrine; it stands alone in its wisdom which is God's wisdom, in its foretelling the future, and in the purity and fluency of its language. Five or more centuries passed before Muslims translated it into other tongues; the earliest Persian attempts wrote the Persian word under the Arabic in the text.

Those, who are not Muslims, cannot endorse these high praises. Even in translation the consecutive reading of several pages of the earlier messages leaves an impression of power. Much of the book is marked by sound common sense, the middle way, for God does not make religion hard for men. Probably this accounts for much of its success. The story of Joseph is the longest and best constructed tale but it shows clearly that Muḥammad, like George Washington, though in another sense, could not tell a story.

The Koran was sent down from the highest heaven in the month of Ramaḍān on the night of power to the house of might; thence it was revealed in the space of twenty years to the prophet.

The titles of the chapters are not part of the original text;

John of Damascus knows of a 'chapter of the camel', a name unknown to Muslims.

It has often been said that there is no clergy or priestly caste in Islam; it is true but there is an element of untruth in the statement. There are of course no sacraments which demand a consecrated priest; any Muslim can perform and preside at any religious act except perhaps the pilgrimage; even in it the signal for starting certain ceremonies is given by the *amīr al-ḥajj*, an official, and anybody can become an official by the grace of God, while the sermon at 'Arafat is reserved to the judge of Mecca, and men of all classes have become judges. When a chance company meets for prayer, the younger man will give place to the elder, the unlettered to the scholar but that is politeness so only indirectly a matter of religion.

Some clerical functions are exercised by the lawyer divines (*faqīh*). When a man is in doubt what to do, he can appeal to a lawyer for guidance, who thus becomes a director of conscience. Because they are the only interpreters of the law, they are the leaders of the community and can influence the progress of religion. Herein they act as clergy. Anyone with brains can become a lawyer, there are no restrictions of birth or race, so learning and personality can make a man a leader. Like the tribal chief, they have little direct but much indirect power. These are the *'ulamā* (plural of *'ālim*), in *sunnī* Islam they correspond to the *mujtahids* of the Shī'a.

CHAPTER II

PILLARS OF ISLAM

THERE are five pillars of Islam, faith, prayer, alms, fasting, and pilgrimage; an attempt was made to add a sixth, the holy war, but it failed. They are treated in detail below.

FAITH

This is summarized in the confession, or the two confessions, as it is sometimes called; "there is no god but God and Muḥammad is the apostle of God." It is belief in one God, the creator. He is separate from the universe and nothing is like Him. He is the absolute monarch; right and wrong are what He has commanded them to be because He has so commanded. The universe is His and He can do what He likes with His own and none can gainsay Him or question His action. In Him is no change; the exercise of His bounty gives Him no pleasure; should He condemn all men to hell, He feels no pain. He is one and there is no hint of anything compound in His perfection. History is the unfolding in time of what has been decreed in eternity. Muḥammad is the last prophet and has brought to men the final revelation which God has for them. This belief is the result of conflicts which are told in more detail in the chapter on the growth of theology.

PRAYER

Worship would be a better name for the ritual expresses adoration not petition. The worshipper must be ritually clean. Some pollutions demand a bath; otherwise it is enough to wash the face, hands, and feet. This ablution is regulated in the minutest detail by religious custom; water must be sucked into the nostrils, the wet fingers put into the ears, and the hands passed over the hair. If no water can be had, sand or dust may be used. The daily prayers are five; before dawn, after noon, in the middle of the afternoon (when a stick casts a shadow its own length), after sunset, and after dark. It seems that this timing is intended to avoid any suggestion of worshipping the sun. Oddly enough, the five prayers are not mentioned in the Koran but they certainly belong to the earliest period of Islam. Each prayer consists of two or more sections with an epilogue. Each section consists of certain phrases and passages from the Koran recited by the worshipper in several attitudes; he stands, squats, bows, and places his forehead on the ground. The morning prayer has two sections, the noon four, the afternoon four, the sunset three, and the night prayer two.

After the ritual a man may add what petitions he pleases. The place where prayer is said must be clean, that is why shoes are left outside the mosque. Some wear goloshes over their boots and leave the goloshes outside. Prayers are said facing Mecca; at first the believers faced Jerusalem; the change was made two years after the emigration to Medina. Mosques are usually built so that the main axis points to Mecca; this was not done with the chief mosque at Tlemcen where the ranks of worshippers run diagonally across the building.

The time of prayer is announced by the voice, by the muezzin crying from the minaret. This call may be as much as half an hour before the prayer is due. A small mosque may have no minaret and the call may be made from the roof or at the door. In the dawn call occur the words, "Prayer is better than sleep", and to all calls the Shī'a adds, "Come to the best of work".

The body must be decently clothed and the head covered. It is meritorious to keep all prayers in the mosque but the only one at all obligatory is the midday prayer on Friday. In early days women attended the mosque and took their places behind the men. This is no longer the custom. Prayer must be said at the proper time, otherwise it is not valid. When praying in the open a man will put something, his shoes or rifle in front of him; this 'fence' is the boundary of his place of prayer, no one will pass between him and it or even close to it.

The following quotations show the value attached to prayer;

the angels in heaven in their prayers go through the same motions as men.

> If anything were better than prayer, the angels would use it in worshipping God.
>
> God has promised to take into paradise him who keeps the five prayers and omits none because he despises what is due to them.
>
> What is the best act? Prayer at the right time.
>
> Prayer is the key of paradise.
>
> The five prayers remove sins as water removes dirt.
>
> Prayers are an expiation for what is done between them so long as a man avoids grave sins.
>
> At the resurrection God will pay no heed to the good deeds of one who has neglected prayer.
>
> Prayer is the prop of religion; he who neglects it has destroyed religion.
>
> Intentional neglect of prayer is unbelief.

The noon prayer on Friday consists of two sections preceded by the sermon. Another prayer of two sections before the sermon is recommended. On the festivals, the feast of sacrifice (*ʿīd al-aḍḥā*) and the breaking of the fast (*ʿīd al-fiṭr*) the sermon follows the prayer. Travellers may postpone a prayer and join it to the next and in the presence of the enemy an army may divide, half standing to arms while half worships—the prayer of fear.

Alms

'Legal alms' or 'religious tax' would be better names for this institution. From the first Muḥammad insisted on charity; later he fixed the minimum by law. As most of the Arabs were pastoral people the law goes into great detail about flocks and herds though much of it is now practically obsolete. To give a few examples; the owner of five to nine camels pays one sheep; of twenty-five to thirty-five camels one female yearling camel; of three hundred camels six female three-year-olds or five two-year-old and two three-year-old cows. The owner of twenty dinars (gold) or two hundred dirhams (silver), which sums were held to be equal, had to pay five per cent on his capital.

In early times the tax camels were collected by the state and used for the wars of conquest. A province was sometimes given the privilege of keeping its alms for distribution within its own borders. It was a matter of debate whether a man should distribute his own alms or whether it should be collected and disbursed by the state. The charity given at the end of Ramaḍān is not part of the alms. Today pious Muslims distribute their alms regardless of taxes paid to the state.

Though the alms were meant for the poor it may be suspected that the state sometimes pleaded poverty.

Two sayings of very different tenor may be quoted:

> A man served God for seventy years and then committed a sin which cancelled the merit of his service. Afterwards he gave a loaf of bread to a poor man, so God pardoned his sin and gave him back the merit of his seventy years' service.
>
> His alms are vain who does not know that his need of the reward for giving is greater than the poor man's need of the gift.

Fasting

Muhammad instituted a fast on the tenth day of the first month soon after his arrival in Medina but a year and a half later he cancelled this and ordained the fast during the whole of the ninth month, Ramaḍān. The method of fasting was this: during the daytime, from the time it was first possible to distinguish a white thread from a black to sunset, the believer must abstain from food, drink, carnal intercourse, and, a modern addition, smoking. Children, pregnant women, the sick, aged, and travellers are excused though travellers are expected to fast the same number of days at some other time. Originally the fast began with the appearance of the new moon—vouched for by two reliable witnesses—and lasted till the next new moon was seen; if clouds prevented this, it was enough to count thirty days. It is now common to regulate the fast by the calendar. It was customary for a crier to go round the town calling on folk to wake in time for a final meal before the day's fast began.

Voluntary fasting was also common; some even fasted continuously. Presumably the fast was intended as an act of worship; now some give it a moral meaning, by it the rich learn hunger and so learn to sympathize with the poor.

It is believed that the fast blots out sins committed during the year. Compare:

> During Ramaḍān the gates of paradise are open, the gates of hell shut, and the devils in chains.
>
> Fasting is the gate to worship.
>
> He who fasts has two delights, breaking his fast and meeting his Lord.

In addition to the abstinence from food a spiritual meaning was read into the fast. Those who observe it are of three grades; the common folk do not yield to their appetites; the elect hold all their members back from sin; the inner circle of the elect avoid all mean desires, all worldly thoughts, and all that is not God.

It is claimed that the fast is a useful discipline; in the heat of an Indian summer it demands great self-control but it does not produce self-control at other times and for other purposes.

It is a sin to fast on a festival.

Pilgrimage

In pagan times two religious rites were connected with Mecca. One consisted in marching seven times round the Ka'ba and seven times between the slight eminences named Ṣafā and Marwā; this was the *'umra* or little pilgrimage; it could be performed at any time but preferably in the seventh month, Rajab. The second was the pilgrimage to 'Arafat, a little hill some sixteen miles to the east of the town. It was celebrated only in the twelfth month, Dhu'l-Ḥijja. Islam has preserved the two but the pilgrimage combines both rites. It is the duty of every Muslim to make the pilgrimage once if certain conditions are fulfilled; he must be of age, of sound mind, and can afford the expense. Pilgrim dress must be worn; for a man this consists of two lengths of unsewn cloth which leave the arms and right shoulder bare; that for a woman has been called a voluminous night-dress. The usual veil is discarded but the face is hidden by a kind of mask. The head is bare but umbrellas are now permitted. The law prefers that this dress should be put on at the starting point but most wait till they are near Mecca; pillars on the main routes to the town show where it must be put on. On arrival the rites of the little pilgrimage are performed. On the seventh day of the month a sermon is delivered in the mosque and the same evening or early next day the pilgrims start for Mina (Muna) where the morning prayer is said. On the ninth they have to be at ʻArafat where they wait from noon till sunset; the time is partly filled by sermons. This wait is the essential; no one who has missed it can call himself a pilgrim (ḥajjī). After sunset comes the rush to Muzdalifa, on the way back to Mecca, where the combined sunset and night prayers are said. The morning prayer of the tenth is said at Muzdalifa and then the crowd moves to Mina where the stoning of the pass, throwing seven stones at each of three pillars, takes place. Here the sacrifices are killed and men have their heads shaved. This ends the tabus which are imposed on pilgrims; normal dress is resumed and it is customary to put on new clothes. After this it is a duty to go to Mecca and march round the Kaʻba. The days from the eleventh to the thirteenth are spent at Mina and each afternoon the pillars are again stoned, each with seven stones. A final ceremony is the circumambulation of the Kaʻba and the march between Ṣafā and Marwā; to do this the pilgrims go to Tanʻīm, on the border of the sacred territory, resume the pilgrim dress. With these exercises the pilgrimage is over.

In the environs of Mecca hunting and the cutting of wood is forbidden; in addition pilgrims may not indulge in sexual intercourse, contract marriages, act as witnesses, while men may not wear rings for ornament, use perfumes, or cut their hair. In spite of the prohibition many make the pilgrimage on charity.

The pilgrim, who avoids vice and wickedness, comes out of his sins as on the day his mother bore him.

The greatest sinner is he who stands on ʻArafat and thinks that God has not forgiven him.

Holy War

The Koran sanctions war against unbelievers. During the conquests everyone took part and later volunteers joined the regular troops. One of the earliest ascetics was a fighter though he refused to take his share of the booty. There was an attempt to exalt the holy war into one of the pillars of religion as is proved by traditions like, "the monkery of my people is the holy war". On the other side are opinions like, "he who takes part in the holy war does so for his own (temporal) gain", and, "the holy war is only one of the duties". The attempt failed, perhaps as a reaction against the behaviour of the Khārijīs. Some of the Mu'tazilīs would have declared any land, where their pet doctrines did not rule, the abode of war.

The schools of law (except Ibn Ḥanbal and following him the Wahhābīs) regarded it as an obligation if certain conditions were fulfilled. These were that unbelievers should begin hostilities, it should be sanctioned by a duly constituted imam, there should be a reasonable hope of success, and the determination to win. As the Shī'a have no visible imam the holy war is not possible for them.

One, who fell in such a war, was a martyr and went straight to paradise where his soul is in a green bird. His corpse was not washed and he was buried in the clothes in which he was killed. Later another meaning was given to this term, "the holy war has ten parts; one is fighting the enemy of Islam, nine are fighting the self". The real war is against sin. There was another extension of meaning, "he who loves, fades away, conceals his love, and dies, is a martyr".

In addition to the 'pillars', other practices have become *sunna*, practically obligatory. It was a common practice to fast on Tuesdays and Thursdays. During Ramaḍān special prayers were performed during the earlier part of the night. They consist of twenty sections divided into groups of four with intervals between the groups, hence the name *tarāwīḥ* (rests). Mālik requires thirty-six sections while the Shī'a demands one thousand sections spread over the month. In these prayers some devout persons repeat the whole Koran once or even more often. At eclipses and during drought there are also special prayers; it happened in Egypt that Muslims, Christians and Jews prayed separately for rain. At the feasts and on other special occasions prayer may be celebrated at a praying place (*muṣallā*) outside the town. In one such the *qibla* was marked by a long low wall with the niche (*miḥrāb*) in the centre; there were no other boundaries. A man can give alms and go on pilgrimage for the benefit of the dead; of course he only earns for himself the merit of doing a pious act. It is possible to make the pilgrimage vicariously and in this case the man, who actually makes the journey, cannot call himself a pilgrim and only earns for himself the merit of having helped a brother Muslim.

They sometimes 'go into retreat', usually as the result of a vow. A man goes alone to a mosque and lives in it for consecutive days, fasting; if the period includes a Friday, the mosque must be one in which the Friday prayer is said. Mālik prefers a minimum of ten days. Should the man break his fast on purpose, he must start the retreat again. No conditions can be attached to a retreat and during it he must not visit the sick, pray over a corpse, or go about his ordinary business. Women also went into retreat.

CHAPTER III

ḤADITH AND SUNNA

WHEN Muḥammad was dead, the attention of the community soon turned to the facts of his life. It may be presumed that some felt a personal interest in them and wanted to know about them for their own sake. Another cause of interest had two aspects; Muḥammad was held to be the model of what a believer ought to be so those, who took their religion seriously, wanted to know every detail of his life that they might imitate him; also it was found that the laws in the Koran were not enough to regulate the life of the young state and that more were needed. It was natural to look to the acts and words of Muḥammad to supply the need. From these causes arose the recording, collection, and classification of the *ḥadīth*, traditions about Muḥammad. Thus the traditions are details in the figure of Muḥammad while the *sunna*, the custom, is the resulting whole, the habit of life which pious Muslims try to make their own. Tradition is the raw material, the custom the finished product, the ideal of the believer.

At first they thought it wrong to write the traditions; this was due to jealousy for the Koran. Therefore it was necessary to learn traditions by word of mouth from those who had learnt them in the same way. This led to much travelling to meet scholars who could impart important traditions. Long after the traditions had been collected in books men still travelled to hear them by word of mouth. Another consequence was that each tradition came to be accompanied by a list of guarantors, beginning with Muḥammad or one of his contemporaries and continuing to the latest recipient. Those who had come into contact with Muḥammad were called Companions and the next generation, who knew him at second-hand, were the Followers. The earliest collections of traditions were private and were called *musnad*; men gathered what they could or those in which they had a special interest. That made by the Umayyad caliph, 'Umar II, is arranged according to the authorities from whom the traditions were received.

It was not long before men began to manufacture traditions. It is hard for us with our ideas of literal accuracy and copyright to appreciate the action of these forgers, a name which they would have been the first to resent. In those days it was no sin to put into a man's mouth words that he might have said or to polish and embellish what he actually had said. One, who believed firmly that he obeyed the prophet, had no hesitation in ascribing his ideas to Muḥammad; if he had not said these things, he ought to have said them. The result is that the sum of tradition represents the history of the first two centuries of Islam.

The men of that time knew that much of the tradition was not authentic and began to criticize. It is said that Bukhārī (†870) examined 600,000 traditions out of which he chose some 7,000 as genuine. Modern scholarship cuts this number down still further. At that time critics paid no attention to the subject matter of a tradition; they considered only the chain of witnesses to it; if that was sound, if the men named in it could have met and were of unblemished character, the tradition was reliable—whatever anachronisms it might contain. Bukhārī's interest was in law so he made the framework of his collection the paragraphs of a legal code and fitted the material into it. For some sections he could find no tradition while the same tradition may occur several times under different headings. The contents is varied; in addition to genuine sayings of Muḥammad and incidents of his life there are bits of folklore, which may be more ancient, quotations and adaptations from the Bible and anticipations of later history.

The pious did not approve of the Umayyad dynasty so it is natural to suppose that traditions, which inculcate unquestioning obedience to the government, were invented to counteract the teaching of the pious, who insisted that obedience was due to God alone. Examples are:

> Muḥammad said, 'Who obeys me, obeys God; who obeys the imam, obeys me; who does not obey me, does not obey God; who does not obey the imam, does not obey me.'

Do not curse rulers; if they do justice, reward is theirs and it is yours to be grateful; if they do wrong, guilt is theirs and it is yours to be patient.

If a crop-eared Abyssinian slave is made ruler over you, obey him.

Pray behind any imam.

The last sentence, besides being political, condemns the censoriousness to which zealots inside and outside Islam are prone.

A series of events was the occasion of the next invention or perversion. Muḥammad had an estate at Fadak; on his death both his family and the state claimed it. The fluctuations of this debate do not concern us but a political meaning was read into it. One tradition says, "A prophet has no heirs; what he leaves is made into a charitable trust". The political meaning is that the descendants of 'Alī have no right to the throne for this right is determined by the community. The Shī'a altered the text, two dots below one letter instead of one dot above, so that it read, "What we have left as a charitable trust cannot be inherited (but everything else can)"; thus getting support for their legitimist claims.

The collection next in importance is that of Muslim (†875); it begins with a long section on faith. These two collections, Bukhārī and Muslim, are named The Two Truthful (*ṣaḥīḥ*) and are more highly esteemed than any others. Three others, which are named *Sunan* (customs) by Abū Dāwūd (†889), Nasā'ī (†915), Ibn Māja (†896) and the *Jāmi'* (collector) of Tirmidhī (†892) run them close in popular esteem. They are known as the Six Books.

These books were all compiled under the rule of the Abbasid caliphs so reports in praise of the Umayyads were excluded. Ibn Ḥanbal made a collection, which he called *Musnad*, more on the lines of the earliest collections and in it are preserved references to the Umayyads which were excluded from the Six Books. Ibn Ḥanbal may have been an impossible person but he had the courage of his convictions.

How knowledge is imparted by God. Revelation (*waḥy*) is given to prophets and has a universal application; it comes in a trance, through hearing a noise, or seeing a figure which speaks;

inspiration (*ilhām*) is an individual message given to saints whose minds are prepared to receive it. It is less than revelation. The Koran is revelation; some traditions are verbally inspired —the so-called holy (*qudsī*)—but in most the words are the prophet's own. The Koran is superior to tradition. A few dared to assert that tradition is superior to the Koran though in practice the agreement of the community decided the interpretation of the Koran. An example of the Koran being contradicted by a tradition is, "It is prescribed to you when any of you is at the point of death, if he leaves goods, that he bequeath equitably to his parents and kindred," whereas the tradition is, "there can be no bequest to an heir". It is objected that there can be no abrogation for the tradition rests on the authority of one man only and so cannot override what is generally known, like the Koran.

As interest in tradition did not arise till after the death of Muḥammad, it is obvious that any which mention tradition are spurious. The prophet said, "Whoever holds his cloak open while I am speaking and then folds it round his body will not forget what I say". One Companion explained that the Helpers were busy with their fields, the Emigrants with their trading, but he himself was poor and so could attend the prophet and therefore he remembered what he said and did. The saying, "In nothing do we see pious men more given to falsehood than in tradition" is ascribed to two men both of whom lived about 800, and many Companions are named as witnesses to "Whoever shall report of me what I have not said, his rest place shall be in hell".

To take only two instances of borrowing from the New Testament, the parable of the sower and that of the labourers in the vineyard have been imitated in tradition, the latter in two forms.

Traditions were divided into three classes with numerous sub-divisions, sound, respectable and weak, the classification depending on the chains of testimony. The chain had to be unbroken, with evidence of contact between the narrators who had to be men of good character, fit to serve as witnesses in a court of law. Any defect or failure in any one of these points lessened the credit of the tradition. One reported by several lines of descent was stronger than one that depended on a single narrator. Some held that the latter could be treated as a basis for action but not for knowledge; a man could rule his own acts by it but could not make a general law from it.

There was jealousy between the various branches of religious knowledge. "The followers of tradition are better off than the theologians who argue, for the heart free from uncertainty is a better Muslim than a breast stuffed with doubt. Argument never produces anything good." "He who seeks religion through theology becomes a heretic."

CHAPTER IV

BELIEFS

Growth of Doctrine

MUHAMMAD was a preacher not a theologian, so it was left to his followers to reduce his ideas to a system. Islam came into being surrounded by religions with developed theologies so its own thought grew as in a forcing house, stimulated by converts who brought into their new faith developed ideas derived from their former religion, and by discussions with Christians and others. Some of the ideas thus introduced into Islam had to be turned out later. The Koran and tradition often speak of God as if He were a man; to take two examples only, "When God created the world He wrote with His hand for Himself, 'My mercy precedes My anger'." and, "He opens the gates of heaven in the last third of the night, stretches out His hand and says, 'Is there none to ask of me that I may give?' He stays like this till dawn." In consequence many thought of God as a body; they asked if the throne supported Him and did He fill it. He had all the limbs of a man, He was a white light in the form of a man and His hair was black light; He was a body but not as other bodies. An early theologian of the Shī'a said that God was a body but not so big as Abū Qubais, a mountain outside Mecca. Mālik expressed the thought of many when he said, "God is on the throne; the fact is known, the manner of it is unknown, faith in it is necessary, enquiry about it is heresy (innovation)".

It is often difficult if not impossible to separate the religious from the political. A political quarrel between 'Alī and the governor of Syria was the occasion of one phase of development. 'Alī claimed to succeed Muḥammad because he was related to him but consented to submit his claim to arbitration. Some of his adherents said that this was an infringement of the sovereignty of God, who was the only judge (whose judgement was given by success or failure in war), and came out (*kharaja*) against him; hence the name Khārijīs. They held that 'Alī had not done his duty as the head of the state and finally came to these conclusions; it is lawful to depose the imam, the head of the state; and further, that any pious Muslim, even a black slave may be the ruler, contradicting the general idea that he must be an Arab of the tribe of Quraish. The Khārijīs went on to claim that they were the only Muslims; some believed, and even put their belief into practice, that all other self-styled Muslims might be killed at sight with their women and children. This raised the question what was a Muslim. The Khārijīs said that the child of Muslim parents was not a Muslim till it was old enough to accept the faith on its own responsibility, that a Muslim was one who upheld the Khārijī creed by word and deed, i.e. by the sword, that there are no venial sins for all sin is rebellion against God and leads to hell, and that faith without works is dead, rather, does not exist. They also raised the problem of what happened to children who died before they could accept Islam. Not all Khārijīs accepted these conclusions in their extreme form but all regarded themselves as the elect of God.

Some urged that men have no right to judge one another, that God is the only judge, He looks on the heart so that faith is all that counts. In the words of a critic, they set faith above works. This attitude was in part a reaction against the Khārijīs and in part acquiescence in the rule of the Umayyads who were called ungodly by the strictest Muslims. They held that anything was better than a breach of the unity of Islam. These people took it for granted that the children of Muslims were Muslims.

The claims of the descendants of 'Alī to leadership were a cause of unrest and extravagant ideas were often associated with them. Many of them were foreign to Islam and are only mentioned here because they turned up in other forms later. Some believed that 'Alī after his death was in the clouds, the thunder was his voice and the lightning his whip; he would return to earth to fill it with righteousness as it is now full of injustice. Some taught that a son of 'Alī, whose mother belonged to the tribe of Ḥanīfa and so was no relative of the prophet, was hidden on a mountain in Arabia, miraculously guarded and fed till he should return and restore all things. The idea of imam is here combined with that of mahdī who will come before the resurrection and the judgement. Twenty-six descendants of 'Alī were held to be imam at different times and several men, who had no connection with him, claimed to inherit this office from one or other of them. These men stood outside Islam but are symptoms of the great religious excitement which flourished during the second century of Islam's history. The prominence of women in some of these movements is a striking fact.

Here are some of the ideas which found votaries. There are two Gods, the greater in heaven, the lesser on earth. God is light in the form of a man and the letters of the alphabet are as the number of his limbs. The first thing to be created was the shadow of Muḥammad; the word shadow seems to be used for what was called later the light of Muḥammad. Ritual practices, heaven, and hell were interpreted as persons; the family of Muḥammad was heaven. There are always two imams, one speaking and one silent. The imams are God. God makes his abode in every beautiful form. God was manifested in five persons, in Muḥammad, his daughter, son-in-law, and two grandsons; opposed to these are five evil contraries and they are the greater for only through their evil is goodness known. Some believed in transmigration and some were professional stranglers, like the Thugs in India, they hurried their enemies to hell and their friends to heaven. It was said that the archangel Gabriel made a mistake and brought to Muḥammad the revelation intended for 'Alī

In Syria and Iraq other forces were at work. At an early date most Muslims believed that God was the absolute ruler of the world; perhaps under Christian influence some questioned this belief and affirmed the freedom of man's will. They were called Qadarīs, from a root meaning power, arrangement; either because they questioned God's arrangement of human affairs or affirmed man's power to live his own life. Some of them suffered martyrdom but they were soon merged in a later school, the Mu'tazilī. Now ideas from Greek philosophy penetrated into Islam and terms like substance and accident became familiar. It became necessary to systematize ideas about the

Koran. It was the word of God; God without a word was unthinkable so the Koran must be eternal and uncreated. The Christian doctrine of the Logos may have helped here. Probably the Koran was the starting point for another doctrine, that of the divine attributes. As God is alive and knows, He must have life, power, knowledge, and speech. His speech is the word, the Koran; this is eternal so the other attributes are also eternal, and, like the Koran, have a being somehow apart from God.

On this stage appeared the Mu'tazilīs; they were not rationalists but they applied reason to religion, within limits. The main tenets are:

God is one, so his attributes have no independent existence.

He is just, he rewards the righteous and punishes the wicked.

He is not the author of evil.

Man is responsible for his actions; he is not a tool in the hand of God.

Reason alone can guide man to a knowledge of God; it agrees with revelation.

It is right to try to justify the ways of God to man.

The Koran is created.

A sinful Muslim is neither a believer nor an unbeliever; he is wicked. Partisan prejudice is manifest in the name given to them by their opponents 'those who deny the attributes'; they denied the quasi-independence of the attributes.

They called themselves the 'people of unity and justice'; variations within the school were many. The doctrines which follow were taught by some of them. There was a tendency to define God by negatives—a tendency not confined to Islam. Muslims were afraid of any statement about God which might seem to limit His infinity; to say that he is wise sets a limit to Him in one direction; He cannot be ignorant so to say that He is not ignorant avoids any suggestion of setting limits to Him. Arabs were often hypnotized by words. There was also a tendency to reduce all the attributes to aspects of knowledge; as He is the creator there is nothing intermediate between thought and act. Similarly, it is said that He has no will, for thought passed at once into action. To the Arabs will was nearer to thought than to power; it was not the mainspring of action but only provided an object to power which, without will, was blind activity; which is inconceivable in God. There is a cause for all His acts, He created men that they might worship Him. Orthodoxy denies this. As all men by the use of reason can know God, there is no room left for faith, belief in God; it is therefore identified with good works. Muḥammad has no right of intercession, much less anyone else. A believer must be able to defend his religion by argument. "If a man knows all about Islam, all the doctrines of Abū Hāshim with their proofs except one, he is an unbeliever." The writer, who quotes this, adds, "We agree with his conclusion but not with his premises".

Doctrines peculiar to individuals or small groups are many. In an attempt to save God from contact with the world of change and decay it was taught that His creative will was an accident not inhering in a substrate, a demiurge like the first reason of the Neo-Platonists. Men came to opposing conclusions. God cannot do evil; He can but He will not. Man is a monad; he is a spirit independent of the body; he is the soul which uses the body like a tool, a combination of soul and body, the body all of which, except the hair and nails, is the agent while life, soul and spirit are accidents in it. Heaven and hell are not yet created for there is as yet no one to occupy them. A prophet may commit sins and may even have been an unbeliever before his call. This is denied. The relative rank of men and angels was debated; some said that men were higher because they could refuse to serve God. The community and religion can exist without an imam; reason and revelation show that he is necessary. Some rejected the theory of atoms. The grace of God gave rise to questions. Could it overrride man's will? If a man believed without the help of it, did he deserve a greater reward than one who was aided by it? Reason cannot prove that the killing of animals for food is lawful; only religion teaches that they may be slaughtered for sacrifice and food. Inaction may merit condemnation; it can merit neither praise nor blame. The Mu'tazilīs had no fear of jinn. As God is just animals, which have suffered in this world, will get compensation in the next.

Under the caliph Ma'mūn this sect was made the state religion and remained so from 833 till 848 but they were as intolerant as any other sect. Aḥmad ibn Ḥanbal was flogged for not accepting the doctrine of the creation of the Koran and prisoners of war were not ransomed from the Byzantines unless they accepted it. Later Mu'tazilīs paid more attention to the workings of the mind and taught that repentance for one sin is not accepted while another is persisted in and it is no use repenting of a sin when one is no longer able to commit it. There was some approach to ideas which were later stamped as orthodox; e.g. reason cannot give any knowledge of the future life, this is the province of revelation.

In 912 Ash'arī, a pupil of the leading Mu'tazilī theologian, broke away from his master and returned to the religion of the old women—to use a phrase coined by a later divine. He taught the doctrine set out in the next section. He employed the method which he had learnt as a Mu'tazilī, in expounding his creed and, though some denounced him as a heretic, his system was at last accepted. No great change was made in theology after his day.

The Creed

There is nothing in Islam corresponding to the Apostles' creed; formulae, which might serve as the beginnings of a creed, occur in the Koran, "O ye who believe, believe in God and His apostle, and the book which He hath sent down to His apostle, and the book which He hath sent down aforetime. Whoever believeth not on God, His angels, His books, His apostles, and on the last day, he verily hath erred with far-gone error"; and in documents quoted in the life of Muḥammad, "those who have embraced Islam, observe prayer, pay the religious tax, obey God and His apostle, and hand over from the booty the fifth for God as well as the portion of the prophet, and adduce warrants for their conversion and turn their backs on the polytheists; for such believe in God". Partial statements of faith occur on tombstones:—

> He testifies that there is no god but God, that He has no partner, that Muḥammad is His servant and His messenger, that the garden is true and the fire true, that he believes in His providence entirely both what is good and bad.
>
> The Koran is the word of God, revealed not created, good and bad both come from Him, Munkar and Nakīr are true, God will be seen without doubt on the day of resurrection.
>
> All that can be worshipped between His throne and the foundation of the earth, except His face, will perish; Islam is what He sent, religion is what He decreed, truth is what He said, justice is what He ordered.

Complete creeds are later and more like treatises on philosophy than creeds.

God is eternal, without beginning and without end, unique for nothing is like Him. He knows by knowledge, lives by life, wills by will, sees by sight, and speaks by His word. These attributes are eternal, inhere in His essence, are not He and not other than He, yet they do not detract from the unity of His essence. He is the absolute lord of what He has created and none can call Him to account for what He does; should He send all creatures to hell, it is not injustice; should He take them all to paradise, it is not wrong. 'Must' does not apply to him. The worship and gratitude of men do not profit Him nor does the unbelief of the infidel hurt Him for all things are His; He willed all that exists, both good and bad, useful and harmful. Right is right and wrong is wrong because God has decreed that they are so. Reason cannot find out these things any more than it can find God. Reason has its place in religion but only within the limits set by revelation. God creates in man the will to act and the act; man acquires the act and this acquisition gives it moral quality. It is affirmed with great emphasis that this doctrine is not determinism, does not reduce man to a machine.

Faith is belief in the mind, confession by the tongue, and good acts done by the members. He who believes in God and His apostle is a believer; faith has seventy-two parts, the highest is the confession, "there is no god but God", and the lowest is removing an obstacle from a path. He, who commits a great sin and dies unrepentant, God will judge him, either pardoning him in His mercy or at the intercession of Muḥammad, or punishing him in hell for a season and then taking him to paradise; for no believer remains in hell for ever. A man may be a believer without being able to give a reason for the faith that is in him.

The word of God is one, being command, prohibition, statement, question, promise and threat, these aspects of it being due to relationships within the word and not to the word itself. What has been revealed by angels to the prophets is a guide to the eternal word; the Koran, the thing indicated, is pre-existent and eternal; the indication, which is the word written, read, or memorized, is created.

The sending of apostles and prophets is possible but not necessary. When God sends prophets and fortifies them by miracles and they invite competition, men must hearken to them and obey them. Wonders worked by saints are real. Belief in a future life depends on revelation.

The theologians developed an atomic theory; space, time, and everything in them consists of indivisible particles, atoms. These are continually perishing and God creates fresh ones to take their place. One result is that there is no order of nature, only custom which God may vary at will. Critics chose Muḥammad as the best position from which to attack this theory. According to it there was not one but myriads of Muḥammads and the one now in heaven is not one of the many who were on earth.

There is no consistent body of teaching about the nature of man; agreement is limited to the fact that he consists of body and something else which will both share in the resurrection. Philosophers accepted the division of the soul into vegetal, animal and rational but this idea did not become popular. The use of terms was not consistent and an elaborate analysis of human nature makes these divisions:

heart (*qalb*) in psychology denotes something superhuman, spiritual; it is the real man, it perceives, knows, is responsible and is the medium for attaining direct knowledge of God:

spirit (*rūḥ*) is 1. a subtle body with its source in the hollow of

the heart whence it spreads through the body by the arteries; 2. is a synonym for the heart:
soul (*nafs*) is 1. the animal soul with its lusts and ambitions, this sense is common in the language of the mystics; 2. man's self or essence:
reason (*'aql*) is 1. the knowledge of what really is; 2. the heart as organ of perception.
secret (*sirr*) is elsewhere used for the essential man stripped of all superfluities.

In another place the soul is called a spiritual substance or atom. This is no scientific psychology.

Many definitions of the soul were given; it is an accident inhering in the body, it is the spirit, it is not the spirit, it is the harmony of the four elements in man, it is life or a being in its own right which controls the body. *Nafs* also means desire consequently soul may take the place of the world and the flesh if not of the devil; the Koran describes it as inciting to evil. On the other hand, the soul at rest (*nafs mutma'inna*) is the highest religious development of which man is capable. The relation of soul and spirit was never defined; one man seems to say that the spirit is joined to the body by the soul. Contradictory ideas were associated with the words; an example has just been given for soul and here is one for spirit. When a man loses a limb, the spirit that was in it retires into what is left of the body. At the questioning in the grave the spirit of a wicked man scatters itself throughout the body because it does not wish to leave it. Some peculiar ideas are found. It is good manners to salute a grave when passing it; the spirit of the dead man comes back to the grave to return the salute. The spirit of the sleeper is in his body for he is alive though not as the waking man is alive for sleep is the brother of death. In like manner, the dead, when the spirit returns to the body, is in an intermediate state between life and death. To Muslims spirit suggests body; a missionary raised a tumult by putting out a placard with, 'God is spirit', translated literally into Arabic.

Next to this analysis of human nature is a fit place to expound the place of faith in man. The Koran sums up the whole duty of man as faith and good works but it does not make the bond between the two clear. It speaks also of increase of faith. Various theories have been mentioned. Without works there is no faith (Khārijī); faith is all important because God sees the heart (Murjī); faith is good works because every man can know God (Mu'tazilī). Then, if a man has faith, it does not matter how he acts; and again, if he confesses God with his lips, it does not matter what he believes. Some argued that faith means belief and there can be no degrees of that.

One answer was that words can have more than one meaning. To a Muslim faith does not mean what it means to a Jew or a Christian and all must admit that they believe in something. On the lips of a Muslim faith means inward belief, outward confession and the way of life which corresponds. Taken in its fullest meaning faith is Islam. This usage was not generally accepted for Islam is taken to be a wider term than faith. Islam is absolute agreement and compliance with the commands of God. Language distinguishes between faith and Islam. Yet there is no faith without Islam and Islam without faith cannot be found. The two are as back and belly. Religion is a noun covering faith and Islam and all the commandments of the law. Ibn Ḥanbal said that all faith was Islam but not all Islam was faith and not every Muslim believed in God for some had turned Muslim for fear of the sword.

The doctrines of Ibn Ḥanbal show what passed for theology in that day. The honourable direction is above, therefore God is above, on the throne. Faith increases by the doing of good works, is diminished by sin, made strong by knowledge and weakened by ignorance. To say that it is created is unbelief but to say that it is uncreated is heresy. God has not commanded men to commit sins but He has arranged for them and made them serve His purposes. The time of a man's death is fixed; if he dies a violent death, he dies at his appointed time. (Some said that death by violence anticipated his appointed time.) When a sinning Muslim is punished in hell, the fire will not singe his face nor burn the limbs which bowed down in prayer for this is forbidden to the fire. Muḥammad's reservoir, from which believers will drink before entering paradise, would stretch from Aden to Oman, on both sides are tents of hollowed pearls, the drinking vessels are in number as the stars, the earth round it is musk, its water is whiter than milk, colder than ice, and sweeter than honey. He who drinks of it will never thirst again.

Theologians are agreed that knowledge is either necessary or acquired. The necessary is intuitive, *a priori*, or based on a general report. Facts of history and geography are known by general report and so are necessary. The acquired is obtained by processes of ratiocination.

Some important facts are known only by revelation. Some say that the first thing which God created was the Pen; this records the word of God and all that is to be in the world. Some say that it is a ray of light and writes of its own volition. It writes on the Preserved Tablet which contains the heavenly Koran, the prototype of that in the hands of men, and the record of all that is and is to be. The throne of God is bigger than the heavens and the earth; two words (*kursi* and *'arsh*) are used in the Koran and there is doubt whether both refer to the throne or one refers to the throne and the other to the footstool. The uncertainty which is found in other religions about the judgement is found in Islam also; sometimes the dead have to wait for the universal judgement to enter paradise and at others entry follows immediately after the questioning in the grave.

When a body was laid in the grave, if the man had been wicked, the walls of the grave closed on him and tortured him. Two angels, Munkar and Nakīr, visited the dead and asked "Who is your God? Who is your apostle? What is your religion?" If the man gave the right answers, God, Muḥammad, and Islam, he was admitted to bliss, otherwise the angels tortured him. The Straight Path is really inconsistent with the idea of a day of judgement. The path, thinner than a hair, sharper than a sword spans hell; believers will pass over it without difficulty but infidels will stumble and fall into the fire.

The terrors of the judgement are described in impressive words. Men will be gathered in a great plain, will seek a hiding place from God and find none, will be tortured by thirst, and all but drowned in their own sweat. Muḥammad told his favourite wife that all would be naked at the judgement. "The women too!" she exclaimed. "On that day each will be so taken up with his own affairs that he will have no thought for others." The records of men's acts will be brought, the believer will receive his in his right hand and the unbeliever will take his in his left. Before admission to paradise the righteous will quench their thirst at a lake outside, then they will enter. Paradise has ten gates, one, the gate of mercy, is never shut. It is said that the poor will enter five hundred years before the rich. The believer is welcomed by angels and the heavenly virgins who are always virgin. Paradise is conceived as a garden where everyone has his mansion in the midst of grateful shade and cooling streams. All is peace and no harsh word disturbs the scene. Speaking to an audience of men Muḥammad did not say much about women in paradise but, when asked by an old woman if there were any old women there, he said "no", meaning that they would all be young again. The description is material but it was not always so understood. A man saw in a dream a dead friend and asked of certain men to be told, "They are eating and drinking before the throne". "What about yourself?" "God knows that I do not care for these things and has granted me to look upon His face." The resurrection of the body is taken for granted; if necessary, the scattered fragments will be gathered together.

Hell is called the Fire and sometimes Jehannum though it has other names; it is controlled by angels appointed for that purpose; some hold that noxious animals go to hell to torment the wicked without themselves feeling any discomfort. One said that God did not send anyone to hell, by its own nature the fire attracted the wicked.

Angels were created from light and form the court of God; it is the general belief that they cannot sin. They vary in rank and function; some do nothing but worship while others attend to the affairs of the world. Muḥammad was evidently familiar with the Jewish legend that God commanded the angels to do obeisance to Adam and that one refused from pride. In the Muslim version he claimed to have been created from the flame of fire and so could not do reverence to an inferior who had been created from earth. Driven out from the service of God, he was allowed to become the adversary of mankind. The reports about things superhuman are full of inconsistences. The story as told by the Shīʿa may be given in more detail. Speaking for himself and the imams, ʿAlī said: "Were it not for us, God would not have created Adam and Eve, paradise and hell, heaven and earth; we must be superior to angels because we knew God before they did. The first thing which God created was our spirits and He made them speak of His unity. Then He created the angels; when they saw that our spirits were one light, they extolled us but we praised God that they might know that we also were created creatures. Then God created Adam and put us in his loins and commanded the angels to do obeisance to him. Their obeisance was worship of God and honour to Adam". This is a reference to the story that God called on all mankind, while they were still in the loins of Adam, to accept Him as their Lord; they accepted and this acceptance is the reason for their obligation to serve God.

Gabriel was the agent of revelation bringing down the Koran from heaven; he did not enter Muḥammad's house without asking permission and sat in front of him like a servant. Every man has his guardian angel. The devil (*al-shaiṭān*) is also called Iblīs and corresponds well enough to the Christian and Jewish ideas. Devil (*shaiṭān*) is often little more than an evil or mischievous jinn. These are of various sorts, some believers and some unbelievers; the former were converted by the preaching of Muḥammad. It is impossible to draw sharp lines of distinction between angels, *shaiṭāns* and jinn.

Prophets are more excellent than angels; Muḥammad is the most excellent of men and after him the caliphs in the order of their succession, Abū Bakr, ʿUmar, ʿUthmān, and ʿAlī. Great stress is laid on the intercession of Muḥammad. Men came to Abraham to ask him to intercede for them with God; he sent them to Moses, Moses sent them on to Jesus, Jesus sent them to Muḥammad who alone has the power of efficacious prayer.

Prophets

God makes His will known to men by prophets of whom there have been 124,000. Any statement of faith will include the sentence, "it is possible and reasonable for Him to send them".

The theory of revelation is static; revelation was first given to Adam and later prophets have repeated the message. Twenty eight are named in the Koran; Adam, Noah, Abraham, Lot, Moses, Isaac, Jacob, Ishmael, Joseph, David, Solomon and Job from the Old Testament. Jonah is the only writing prophet mentioned. From the New Testament are Jesus, Zacharias and John the Baptist. Some were sent to Arabia, Hūd to 'Ād, a people of whom nothing is known, Ṣāliḥ to Thamūd, a well-known Nabataean tribe, and Shu'aib, who has been identified both with Jethro and Hobab (Numbers x, 29), to Midian. Luqmān, a mysterious figure who is rather like Aesop, became a hero of popular story. He was a tailor or a carpenter or a herdsman or an Aethiop with thick lips and split feet. He lived for 560 years, seven times an eagle's life. Idrīs is usually identified with Enoch though the evidence is weak; it has been suggested that he is Andreas, the cook of Alexander the Great in the legend.

There are two classes of prophets; those who introduced a new law including religious, legal, and social ordinances, are also called apostles. They are Adam, Noah, Abraham, Moses, Jesus and Muḥammad. The others only repeated the message of their predecessors. A hundred and four revealed books have been given to prophets; ten each to Adam and Abraham, fifty to Seth, thirty to Enoch, one to Moses (the Law—Tawrāt), one to David (Zabūr—Psalms), one to Jesus (Gospel—Injīl), and the Koran to Muḥammad. The contents of all these books is the same; differences are due to the fact that the Jews and Christians have falsified their books. It is nowhere stated when this falsification took place, whether before or after the coming of Muḥammad. Khaḍir is not named in the Koran but there is a story about a wise and righteous servant of God who is certainly he. The origin of this person is to be sought in Babylonian, Greek and Hebrew legend. There are hints that he was once a vegetation god. He lives for ever, is the patron of sailors, and helps all men when in straits; he lives in Jerusalem and every Friday says the midday prayer in the mosques of Mecca, Medina, Jerusalem, Qubā and the Mount of Olives.

Muslims believe in the earlier prophets because Muḥammad has authenticated them. The accepted belief is that they cannot sin. The name of a prophet is always followed by the benediction, "on him and on our prophet be peace". Jesus was not crucified. Muḥammad is called the seal of the prophets, which is taken to mean that there can be no prophet after him for with him God has given men the perfect religion. A modern writer puts Muḥammad at the centre of religion; his is the last word in faith; he is the first, the last, the gatherer (of men at the judgement), the beloved in whom God is well pleased to whom He has granted the right of intercession; God said to him, "I shall not be mentioned unless you are mentioned with Me, I have made you the first of the prophets to be created and the last to be sent". The 'light of Muḥammad' is described in the chapter on mysticism.

Mahdī

The word means 'guided' but, as all men are led by God, it comes to mean one who stands in a specially close relation to Him. It may be noted that it is a favourite name for converts to Islam. It was applied as a title of respect to the four orthodox caliphs, and to some of the Umayyads by their admirers. In its technical religious sense it was given to a son of 'Alī, Muḥammad the son of the woman of the tribe of Ḥanīfa, though he himself would have nothing to do with it. After his death he was believed to be hidden on a mountain in Arabia, miraculously fed and guarded, till he should return to rule in righteousness. Belief in the return was common especially among the extreme Shī'a; sometimes it was the return of the imam as mahdī, sometimes of the whole people. The mahdī is the ruler who will restore all things and usher in the golden age. There was talk of a Sufyānī mahdī, a representative of the elder branch of the Umayyads, who would take vengeance on the Abbasids and restore the fortunes of his family. (The name is derived from Abū Sufyān the ancestor of the family.) This shadowy figure is all that remains of a 'lost bit of Muslim history'. The southern Arabs in their turn looked for a Qaḥṭānī mahdī to restore the ancient glory of that branch of the nation.

Sunnī Muslims regarded the community as capable of governing itself; working on the basis of Koran, *sunna*, and analogy, scholars could unite the community in an agreement which would meet any emergency; there was no need of an inspired teacher to guide them. While the mahdī is an essential element of religion to the Shī'a, to the *Sunnīs* he is a piece of popular religion who is ignored, to a great extent, by theologians and the learned. He is one of the figures who will herald the end of the world. The general scheme was suggested by the Jewish ideas called the 'woes of the Messiah'; Muslims speak of the 'determinants of the Hour'. The world will go from bad to worse till wickedness is universal. Then the sun will rise in the west and there will be three eclipses, in the west, the east, and Arabia; God and Magog will break through Alexander's wall and overrun the earth; Dajjāl, a gigantic king living on an island in the Indian ocean, will appear somewhere in Asia and in forty days will conquer the world; Jesus and the mahdī will come down to earth; Jesus will help the mahdī to kill Dajjāl, kill all swine, and will re-establish the Muslim faith; Jesus will pray behind the mahdī who will rule for seven, eight, or nine years of peace and plenty when gold will be as the dust of the earth. The mahdī will die and prayers be said over him.

It is hopeless to try to reduce these ideas to a system; while most expect the mahdī to come from the east a Spanish writer makes him appear in the west; one version makes him kill the Sufyānī and many traditions make him a descendant of Muḥammad. "He who does not believe in the mahdī is an infidel while he who does not believe in Dajjāl is a liar." Religious men like Ghazālī ignored the mahdi and concentrated on the judgement and its consequences, trying to awaken their hearers' conscience. A belief in the hidden imam, who would return as the mahdī, was common to all sects of the Shī'a; 'Abdullāh ibn Saba is said to have expected the return of 'Alī, "if you bring us his brain in a hundred bags we shall not believe that he is dead". The idea of 'return' was in the air; some expected the return of Abū Muslim, the murdered architect of Abbasid success; the followers of Bihfarīd, who tried without success to lead a national resistance against Islam, expected his return; three hundred years later devotees of Ḥallāj visited the spot in Baghdad where he was executed and expected his return there. The Shī'a, always disappointed in its hopes of worldly success, turned naturally to the future and the return of the imam as mahdī. The twelfth imam disappeared as a child; for some seventy years he was represented on earth by agents, this is the lesser concealment; then began the greater concealment but even now he is the 'Lord of the age' and makes his will known to the faithful. A letter placed on the grave of an imam or thrown into the sea will reach him and be answered. For one he solved legal difficulties; for another he answered prayer so that a man could boast that he had been begotten at the direct intervention of the 'Lord of the age'. Earthly rulers act in his name and as his deputies. When a parliament was set up in Persia the constitution spoke of "the agreement and approval of the imam of the age—may God hasten his coming". And in 1908 a manifesto in favour of the constitution said, "Perhaps you have not heard of the decision of the divines of the holy city of Najaf, a clear and unambiguous decision, that any one who opposes the constitution is as one who draws the sword against the imam of the age (the hidden mahdī), may God grant you the joy of his return".

This belief is an essential part of the faith; the mahdī is known by several names. Here is an extract from a creed:

> We believe that the earth cannot be without the Proof of God to His creatures . . . that the Proof of God in His earth and His vicegerent among His slaves in this age of ours is the Upholder (of the law of God), the Expected One. . . . He it is whom God will make victorious over the whole world until from every place the call to prayer will be heard, and all religion will belong entirely to God. . . . And we believe that there can be no other Upholder than he; he may live in the state of occultation (as long as he likes); and were he to live in the state of occultation for the space of the existence of this world, there would nevertheless be no Upholder other than he. For the prophet and the imams have indicated him by his name and his descent; him they appointed as their successor and of him they gave glad tidings.

Sunnīs made fun of this belief, enlarged on the impossibility of any one living so long, pointed out that the hidden imam was a child when he went into concealment and so unfit to be imam, who must be an adult. Furthermore he does not fulfil the condition of having the same name as the prophet, Muḥammad son of 'Abdullāh.

All rebellions justified themselves by claiming to be a return to the Koran and *sunna*; in some the leader claimed to be the mahdī. To mention only a few; the best known is the founder of the Fatimid dynasty in Egypt; at the end of the fifteenth century one appeared in Ahmadabad. His followers still exist with peculiar rites for marriages and funerals. Their opponents say that they neither do penitence for their sins nor pray for their dead because the mahdī has come. In England we do not need to be reminded of the mahdī in the Sudan. A modern rebel in Morocco claimed to be a saint, spoke of divine mysteries and proclaimed the coming of the 'lord of the age'.

Philosophy

Something must be said about the relations between religion and philosophy. Strictly speaking there is no such thing as Muslim philosophy; the nearest approach to it is the orthodox system of theology, at which the philosophers laughed. Theologians retaliated by calling their critics infidels. Philosophy was an esoteric discipline not to be published to those unworthy of it, something to be taught behind closed doors to the elect. Averroes (Ibn Rushd) insists that the crowd cannot appreciate proof; he divides men into three groups, the crowd, those who can appreciate a debating argument, and the elect who understand real proof. The arguments used with the third class must not be addressed to the second and still less to the crowd. Ghazālī wrote for a wider audience than professional scholars but he gave one pamphlet the title, "What may be given only in small measure to those unworthy of it". Averroes goes further and says that the crowd should not read any of Ghazālī's books. It is not surprising that the theologians smelt evil behind this secrecy; heresy hunts were frequent, especially in Spain.

Philosophy was a brand of neo-Platonism built on a foundation of Aristotle. The common charge against it was that it taught that the world was eternal, that God knew only universals not particulars, and that it denied the resurrection of the body. It is easy to understand that theologians, who were accustomed to think of the soul as an accident in the body, were startled when Avicenna (†1037) spoke of soul-substance. His psychology too must have shocked them. He said that the soul is hindered by the body. When it leaves the body, it is kept back by the qualities it has derived from the body. The weaker these are, the less will it be careless of its perfection and kept back from the place where it will find bliss. The constitution of the body is opposed to the soul-substance and damages it, diverting it from bliss. When it leaves the body, it perceives this opposition and suffers from it. The resultant pain is not inevitable but accidental and, therefore, does not endure; it stops when the actions, which produced it, stop. This pain is punishment which is not lasting but gradually disappears till the soul is pure and attains the bliss which belongs to it. The simple soul, naturally disposed to goodness, which has acquired neither the desire for perfection nor the evil habits of the body, goes to the wide mercy of God and a kind of rest. If it has acquired these evil habits and nothing else, it is punished severely by the loss of the body and its inability to obtain its desires because the means to obtain them has been destroyed. Whether from conviction or prudence Avicenna finds a place for prophets in his system. He adopts the assumption common in Islam that all useful knowledge is based on revelation. He argues thus: man is a social animal therefore he needs a law to live by. This law can only be given by a man, by one who brings it from God. Such a man is fitted by his constitution to receive the law from God; but such a constitution occurs very seldom so prophets come at long intervals in the life of the world. Men would forget the teaching of the prophet in a generation or two unless they were reminded of it, so the prophet establishes the forms of religion and the most important of these is the daily prayer which keeps God constantly before men and reminds them that purity and humility will bring them the blessings of this world and the next.

Ghazāli (†1111) turned the tables on the philosophers and showed that they could not prove the ideas which Islam condemned and further that they could not prove the existence of one God, the creator. Although he believed that the soul is a spiritual substance, he affirmed that philosophy could not prove it. For him the universe is in three layers, the physical world which is that of *mulk* (possession, kingship), that of *malakūt* (sovereignty, glory) which is described somewhere as above the throne of God, and that of *jabarūt* (power) which lies between the other two. Frontiers in this spiritual or mystical geography fluctuate with the writer. The soul belongs to the world of *jabarūt*. One definition admits only two layers; *mulk* is the exoteric aspect of being and *malakūt* the esoteric.

Averroes (†1198) was a lawyer as well as a philosopher so, when he wrote on theology, he may have been anxious to display his orthodoxy. He says that the task of philosophy is to consider facts in so far as they point to a creator; this is only reducing the practice of the Koran to a system. Revelation is the source of much human knowledge for "if the sciences of mechanics and astronomy did not exist, no one could learn all that is now known of them except by revelation". Reason does not contradict revelation. The crowd cannot imagine anything that is not body and thinks that what it cannot imagine does not exist. So the Koran speaks to them in words they can understand and calls God light, the most widely known object in the world. Naturally the Koran says also that men will see God in the hereafter. Muḥammad said, "We are told to speak to men according to the measure of their intelligence". So the Koran, if rightly understood, is nearer to reason than the allegorical interpretations of it. If reason contradicts the Koran, then it must be interpreted; but if interpretation of one part is needed, the truth is stated plainly elsewhere. However, if two verses or sets of verses contradict each other, reason must decide between them. Philosophy agrees with Islam. From one point of view the universe is created, from another it is eternal; the Koran emphasizes the creation but admits that being and time are eternal. The terms universal and particular do not apply to God's knowledge for man's knowledge is derived from things whereas His knowledge causes them.

The statements made by revelation about the future life are either literal or metaphorical; the followers of Ash'arī hold that they are descriptions of what is possible and so do not need interpretation; according to Averroes they are addressed to the crowd in terms it can understand. Any interpretation can only be directed to scholars and must not be divulged to the crowd.

The arguments for the being of God are providence and creation. Providence is displayed in the fact that the world is planned with a view to man and this plan is essential. Everything in the world is invented and an invention needs an inventor; nature is a manufactured article. Averroes attacks theologians for their methods. Many of the premises on which they built their system are sophisms which contradict experience, e.g. that accidents endure only for one unit of time and are continually being renewed. They establish belief in God on reason; He is the end of a chain of argument; He is the creator of the phenomenal world because it is made up of compounds and because they are composed of atoms. This argument cannot be understood by intelligent men, is not conclusive and does not prove God. In another place he says that the arguments of theology do not rest on the wisdom of God but on contingency. If a thing is possible, reason says that it may exist in one form or the opposite of that form; that it has one of the two is due to action from outside, from God. Obviously this argument does not rest on the wisdom of God or His providence. Theology wished to avoid recognizing causes other than God but he, who denies the sequence of cause and effect, denies the wise creator.

On man's activity he says, God has created for us powers by which we can acquire opposites. The acquisition of one of these opposites is possible only by the help of causes outside ourselves which He has put at our service. Our acts are done by our will and the congruence of external forces. These external causes do not only complete the acts which we will to do but are the cause that we will one of two alternatives. For will is desire which arises in us from imagination or belief; this belief is not optional but comes to us from without. Goodness and righteousness cannot exist without the possibility of evil, so Averroes dares to say that God creates evil for the sake of good. God cannot do the impossible.

The intellect is distinguished from the soul. The intellect is abstract and exists only when it is united with the universal active intellect; in man it is only a possibility of receiving ideas from the active intellect. The soul is the motive power which causes life and growth; it is form to the matter of the body. It remains as an individual after the death of the body.

CHAPTER V

LAW

THE Koran contains some laws, e.g. on inheritance, marriage, interest, debt, and the duties of witnesses though it is obvious that the community continued to be ruled by Arab custom so long as this was not opposed to Islam, with appeal to Muḥammad in cases of doubt. After his death his place was taken by records of his words and acts. These were at first oral and out of them was built up the *sunna*. What divides Muslim law from other systems is the fact that it is largely not a natural growth from the life of the community but was elaborated by theorists. In the reign of the third caliph, if not earlier, opposition between religion and the state appeared, which is not surprising; religion developed its own system while condemning the government though not working against it. Money was the cause of the first breach, The state enforced in the provinces the taxes which had been paid to the previous rulers before the conquest; these were not sanctioned by the Koran. A special word (*maks*) was used to denote them and pious men refused appointment as collectors of these taxes. (Centuries later the first act of every new ruler was to repeal these taxes.) Not long after came refusals to act as judge with the implied condemnation of the government.

For the early centuries historians have little to say about the administration of justice so only occasionally is the process by which the Government determined law visible. A judge in Egypt consulted 'Umar II on knotty problems and a later caliph sent instructions on a point of law. Blood-money is an instructive example of what might happen. One school of thought held that the blood-money for a Christian or a Jew, who was killed, was the same as that for a Muslim; another school held that it was only the half. The difference derives from the action of the first Umayyad caliph who extracted the full sum but kept half for the treasury, in other words himself, and gave the remainder to the family of the dead Christian.

The story is that Muḥammad sent a man as governor to Yemen and asked him on what he would base his judgements. "On what is in the book of God." "If that fails you?" "On judgements given by the prophet." "If they fail you?" "I will use my intelligence and not fail." The story may be apocryphal but it is what happened many times and in many places. An obvious use of common sense was to decide a fresh case on the ground of its likeness to an earlier one.

Roman law had ruled in the provinces conquered from Byzantium so it is not surprising that the young state incorporated some of its practices. Some may even have penetrated Arabia before the rise of Islam, following in the track of trade. Common to both Roman and Muslim law is the principle that the plaintiff must bring proof while the defendant may take an oath; Roman also is the idea, admitted by one school of Muslims, that guardianship may last till the ward reaches the age of twenty-five. It has been argued that the classing under one head of booty taken in war, what comes out of the sea, treasure trove, and mines is due to the fact that in Roman these are all forms of *occupatio*.

Pious men worked out for themselves a Muslim scheme of life and such men might be called in to advise others. When they first went outside the Koran and *sunna* to devise laws for themselves and the community they spoke freely of 'using their own judgement' and the term used comes from a root meaning sight, physical or mental. The word they used is restricted to mental sight and is usually translated in this connection 'opinion' though 'common sense' is a fit rendering. The earliest scheme to win general recognition was that of Abū Ḥanīfa (†767), a Persian who formed his system in Iraq. None of his books, if he ever wrote any, have come down to us and his system exists only as it was elaborated by his disciples. He was unique in allowing the use of Persian in worship and he made no secret of the fact that he did not bother much about prophetic authority for his rulings but trusted to common sense. It was felt that this made too high a claim for the human law-maker and some less arrogant term was wanted. Abū Ḥanīfa or his school adopted approval (*istiḥsān*) which might mean 'thinking equitable'. This in its turn was found wanting.

About the same time Mālik ibn Anas (†795) developed another system in Medina. Coming from the town of Muḥammad there is much emphasis on tradition but he admitted the use of common sense though he spoke of 'suitability' (*istiṣlāḥ*) which suggests that the proposal is an improvement on what has gone before. The traditions, on which he based his decisions, are collected in the *Muwaṭṭā* but for many paragraphs of the law there are none and the general agreement of the learned is the basis of his ruling. He merely reduced to strict form the common practice of Medina. Another term to be favoured was 'association' (*istiṣḥāb*); the proposed law was not new at all, it was an extension of an existing one into a new sphere.

Not long after, Shāfi'ī (†820) founded another school which in theory was the mean between the first two; he recognized the part to be played by common sense but set narrower limits to its exercise. It was felt that this was the happy mean between the irresponsibility of Iraq and the stiffness of Medina. "The adherents of tradition could not argue and so refute the advocates of common sense; the energies of the advocates of common sense were spent in defending their conclusions. Then came Shāfi'ī, who knew the Koran and tradition, also the principles of law and proof, and was strong in debate. He converted most of the supporters of common sense." Actually there is little difference between the three schools; their conclusions are not always the same but the method is one with slight changes of emphasis. All use tradition and all employ intelligence but they have different names for the latter.

Shāfi'ī described his procedure as 'analogy' (*qiyās*); the proposed ruling was on the same lines as earlier, similar situations called for similar treatment; in this way he defended his proposals. He followed also the agreement of the community as a whole, going further than Mālik who had followed the agreement of Medina. There are several types of analogy.

1. That based on a cause and so is categorical for reason cannot approve a refusal to accept it. The example given is the punishment of a disrespectful, disobedient son with stripes.

2. That based on demonstration (*dalāla*); it is suggestive and not categorical. An example is the property of a minor. It is as liable as that of an adult to the legal alms and therefore should pay the tax. It is reasonable to accept this argument though Abū Ḥanīfa did not.

3. That based on likeness; it concerns a conclusion which hesitates between two principles and is finally attached to the one it more nearly resembles. The example is a slave who is killed. His value can be considered that of a free man, in so far as he is a man, or of an animal, in so far as he is a chattel. The case is nearer to property than to the free man because the slave can be sold and inherited.

Very different was the fourth school, that of Ibn Ḥanbal (†855). He was primarily a student of tradition and clung to the crude ideas which were common in the early days of Islam. He formulated no code but gave his opinion on many questions and these were set in order by his disciples. As a basis for his decisions he accepted tradition and legal opinions delivered by the Companions. Faced with a choice of decisions he took that which was closest to the Koran and the *sunna*. If there were two opinions of equal value, he gave two decisions. If the only tradition bearing on the problem was weak, he allowed analogy but did not like decisions which were not based on tradition. He resisted all innovations as strenuously as he resisted the theology of the Mu‘tazilīs and Ash‘arī. These four schools are all equally orthodox and every *sunnī* Muslim belongs to one of them. It is reported that Hārūn Rashīd wished to make the *Muwaṭṭa* the code for the empire but Mālik refused. This attitude is caught in a tradition, "the differences of my community are blessings to them". Other teachers flourished and gathered disciples but these schools soon died out, eclipsed by the greater; they were part of the turbulent life of the second century and were part of the growing pains of Islam. One deserves mention, the Ẓāhirī which carried to an extreme the ideas of Ibn Ḥanbal; religion and the sacred law are divine, whereas analogy can only give a law based on reason. The Koran and tradition were the only basis for law and had to be taken in their literal sense without any explaining away, any interpretation to make the text mean other than what it obviously did mean. The school forbade asking the reason for a rule and then extending the rule to cases where the same reason held. Agreement was that of the earliest Muslims only. Naturally many traditions were required with the result that the school was accused of accepting spurious traditions which every one else rejected. In spite of its principles, it was sometimes more lax than the others. It is forbidden to use gold and silver vessels for eating and drinking; the Ẓāhirīs forbade them for drinking only because the tradition does not mention eating. They regarded wine as unclean but not forbidden. Opponents of analogy said that the devil was the first to use it when he refused to bow down to Adam on the ground that he was created from fire and Adam from earth.

As a result of the practice of the schools Muslim law is based on the Koran, the traditions, analogy, and the agreement of the community. Analogy sometimes took the form of seeking the reason for a law. This anecdote is unhistorical. When Taif was conquered and the inhabitants accepted Islam, one man had ten wives; he was told to keep four and divorce six. The lawyers of Medina held that he might divorce any six he liked; those of ʿIraq held that he must keep those whom he had first married for, according to Muslim law, he had never been married to the others. Islam, like all religions, is conservative and 'innovation' is one name for heresy; yet if a practice or belief has been adopted by the community, it is good Islam. This contradiction can lead to odd results. Ibn Taimiya spent his life and suffered imprisonment for protesting against the worship of saints yet hosts of those, who rejected his teaching and adored saints, attended his funeral. The religion has been able to change and adapt itself to new conditions.

The doctrine of the agreement of the community has, of course, been crystallized in a tradition, "my community will not agree on what is wrong". In theory agreement is the agreement of the lawyers; but as there is no supreme legislative body, it could only come about by individuals gathering a following and these finding themselves of one opinion. The opinions of the common people were ruled out. This theory was not always upheld by experience.

Agreement may come from above by a decision of scholars

or from below by the recognition of what is done or believed by the people. An example of the former is the resolution of the antagonism between the mystics and the theologians. Ghazālī showed that a man might be a good Muslim and a mystic and his teaching has become part of Islam. A clear example of the victory of the common man over the scholar is the worship of saints. Theology affirms that God is the only creator and ruler of the world and the one agent in it, yet common folk take their prayers to saints to whom they even offer sacrifices. It has been said that for many Muslims God is far off and negligible whereas the local saint is close at hand and jealous; a man will swear falsely by God though he would not dare to insult the local or tribal saint by so doing. It is true that these examples are not taken from law, in the English sense of the word; India, however, shows how circumstances triumphed over theory in law. When the Muslims conquered northern India, they found the inhabitants worshipping idols. There is no place for idolaters in a Muslim state yet, faced with the impossibility of killing off the whole population, the conquerors admitted them to the privileges of the 'people of the book'. Akbar even took Hindu wives. The treatment of Zoroastrians as 'people of the book' is an earlier and only less striking example of the same process.

The study of the bases of law, Koran, *sunna*, analogy and the agreement of the community (*ijmā*ʿ) became a separate discipline the subject matter of which is the derivation of law from reasonable suppositions. It deals with law under this aspect only. It starts with words and sentences, treating their meaning under three heads, natural, rational and prescriptive or positive. A positive meaning is one attached arbitrarily to a word for general convenience. An attempt was made to elevate custom to the rank of a fifth base but it failed though often custom ruled in practice. Ibn Ḥanbal and the Wahhābīs restrict agreement to that of the Companions. The Khārijīs restrict it to members of their own sect but demand unanimity.

The Shīʿa admits the Koran and *sunna* as bases but the latter includes that of the twelve imams whose infallible authority guarantees the law in the same way as the agreement of the *sunnīs*. They have their own collections of traditions.

Having the imam they need no further bases. The historical school limits deductions as far as possible and derives its law from the traditions of the imams; the theoretical school recognizes reason as a base but this is only another name for analogy. Lastly there is the agreement of the majority of divines since the occultation. While *sunna* can annul *sunna* and even the Koran, agreement can only supersede tradition.

When the four schools were well established, it was felt that an end had been reached; henceforth no change was possible. No one could begin again from the beginning and start a fresh codification, create a new school. All that was left for future scholars was to develop the principles which they had received. In the jargon of the schools there could be no new 'roots' only 'branches'. Existing laws could be extended or adapted to new needs and circumstances but there could be no new way of looking at things as a whole. The day of the *mujtahid* was over; the founders of the schools were *mujtahids*, were entitled to deal with principles and exert an independent judgement; their successors could not deal with principles and could use their judgement only within the limits set by the rules of the school. The result was that the study of law degenerated into casuistry; the books, which were written, lost all claim to be original works, they were commentaries on earlier works or glosses on the commentaries. Books were written about legal tricks. Thus Hārūn Rashīd had promised a slave girl that he would neither give her away nor sell her; he grew tired of her so his court lawyer provided a way out of his dilemma; he sold half of her and gave the other half away.

Theologians divided acts into good and bad which they called obediences and disobediences, underlining the fact that the moral law is established by God. Bad deeds, sins, were grave or venial, the venial can be atoned for by good deeds or by the punctual observance of religious observances, especially prayer. All sins require repentance but God's reaction to sin is incalculable, He may forgive the grave and punish the venial. One tradition says that thoughts, which are not translated into action, are not sinful. This contradicts the usual emphasis laid on intention; there is a story that a man, who tried to commit murder but only wounded his victim, was punished according to the law of retaliation whereas another who had contemplated murder, was put to death.

The law divided actions into five classes:

1. commanded (*farḍ*, *wājib*)
2. approved (*mandūb*, *mustaḥabb*)
3. indifferent (*mubāḥ*)
4. disliked, condemned (*makrūh*)
5. forbidden (*ḥarām*)

The first class has two divisions; those like prayer which are incumbent on all Muslims and those, like the practice of medicine, which need only be performed in sufficient quantity to meet the needs of the community.

From the first the ruler was the chief judge; when a judicial system was set up, he still acted as judge outside the normal forms of law. The caliph or his representative 'sat for complaints'. This was not only a court of appeal; anyone who could not get justice in the ordinary way—because his adversary was too powerful or was a servant of the ruler—could appear before this tribunal. The early Umayyad caliphs undertook this duty in person but later it was delegated to a deputy. A judge was usually associated with him to make sure that the law was observed. At the present day Ibn Sa'ūd maintains this custom of public audience and anyone who feels himself wronged can approach him for justice.

Local customs, which were not felt to be contrary to religion, have often been adopted into law. Perhaps it was impossible to eradicate them. Thus a customer might ask a craftsman to make an article to a fixed specification at a fixed price; this was allowed though it contradicted the principle that a man may not sell what he does not possess. The lawyers of Balkh allowed a man to give yarn to a weaver who would keep one third of it as his pay. Some allowed the sale of the total produce of an orchard though all the fruit might not be ripe at the same time. It was held essential that one, who set up as an authority on law, must know the customs of the trades of the country where he proposed to practise. It is laid down in the Koran that a homicide shall pay blood-money and set free a slave. Tribes on the western border of Egypt ask £300 as blood-money but some demand £400; the extra hundred is the substitute for a woman who was given to the tribe of the dead man to give birth to a man to replace the one slain. The custom of giving a woman is also found in Iraq.

The force of custom is shown in questions of inheritance. The law is laid down in detail in the Koran; the main points to notice here are that the widow receives a share of her husband's estate, and daughters inherit though a female usually gets half the share of a male. In parts of Palestine, North Africa, and in many places in India daughters do not inherit; sometimes they are only forbidden to inherit land. In some tribes in the Punjab exogamy rules, a woman must marry outside the clan but property cannot leave it so she cannot inherit from her father. In parts of Sumatra where exogamy and matriarchy prevail, a man's personal estate goes to his nearest relative on the mother's side, the rest of the property remaining with the widow and going to her children after her. Some converts from Hinduism do not approve of the re-marriage of widows.

Customs which have received the force of law are called '*āda* or '*urf* and from the latter word the adjective '*urfī* has been formed. Attempts have been made to get custom recognized as one of the bases of law. One writer on constitutional law admits that the head of the state was appointed sometimes according to law and sometimes according to custom. An historian states that in Egypt two systems ruled, administered by two sets of officials; Muslim law administered by the judge, and Tatar law, which had been introduced by the mamlukes, administered by palace officials. This was concerned with government business, the fiefs of the soldiers and disputes among them. Later it trespassed on the province of the judge by usurping all jurisdiction connected with private debts because of complaints made by foreign merchants to the sultan.

The status of customary law has been thus defined. The continued application of customary law after the custom has changed is contrary to 'agreement' and shows ignorance of religion for new laws should be made to fit the new customs. Scholars are agreed on this.

Another example of the mixed character of Muslim practice

comes from South Arabia. To the north-east of Aden is a class of men who are hereditary and appointed judges. The chief of these is the hereditary judge or *manqad*; the word is derived from a root meaning 'to pick out, investigate'. He is elected from one family. The family itself has great influence in local public affairs, but only its elected head styles himself a *manqad*, and he has the title of *manqad al-manāqid*, or 'Judge of judges'. Once elected he, without consulting anyone, appoints four or five other *manqads*. He does not appoint them from his own family, but from outside, and his choice is not limited to any class or tribe. These men perform the duties of a final court of appeal. Their judgements are given according to the widest possible code, which they describe as 'Muslim law, custom, and right'. Once having put his case to a *manqad*, no tribesman would either withdraw it or refuse to abide by the *manqad's* decision. To do so would be to forfeit this tribal honour by committing a great shame. Consequently their judgements in disputes are only sought when all other courts have failed. When a chief *manqad* dies and a new one is elected by the family, all other *manqads* are suspended until they are confirmed by the new chief *manqad*.

The law covered the whole of life so, beside ordinary legal work, lawyers were consulted by men with troublesome consciences. In later times lawyers were given all sorts of posts; judges turn up as commanders of armies. Consequently the easiest road to advancement for a bright lad was the study of law. It must be remembered that social distinctions were fluid; indeed it might be said that there were only two classes in the state, the ruler and the ruled. The aristocracy consisted of officials and these lived only at the will of the ruler. The stock example is this:

> I saw in the memoranda of the treasurer, '400,000 dinars for a robe of honour for Ja'far the Barmakī'; a few days later I saw below it, '10 *kīrāṭ* for oil and reeds for burning the body of Ja'far'. (Ten *kīrāṭ* is probably half a dinar.)

But in this devotion to the study of law the spirit was lost and attention was concentrated on the letter; this reacted on religion.

Ghazālī made a name for himself as a teacher of law but gave it up after passing through a spiritual crisis and devoted himself to awakening the religious spirit; in so doing he directed his fiercest invectives and bitterest sarcasm against the lawyers.

The bedouin on the borders of Egypt recognize no law but their own. If one of them were put in prison under Egyptian law, on coming out of gaol he would be punished by his fellow tribesmen. There the chiefs are the judges. Among the bedouin of Syria justice is not the business of the chiefs but of men famed for their intelligence, memory, and knowledge of tradition. This office is often hereditary. The chief may try to get an agreed solution of a quarrel; if he fails, the judge is called in. Among the Shammar are four well-known judges; one of these will also preside at the trial by ordeal, which usually takes the form of licking a red-hot iron ladle.

In all countries, which formed part of the Ottoman Empire (except Arabia), modern codes of penal and commercial law have taken the place of Muslim law which now deals only with personal status. The same has happened in India. Strictly speaking Islam does not allow international law to exist. The world is divided into two parts; the abode of peace where Islam rules under the one caliph; the abode of war where Islam does not rule, where fighting is always meritorious and 'war is deceit'.

Malaya offers a good example of customary law. The Malays, as good Muslims, profess to accept the legal teachings of Islam even where those teachings conflict with the local customs; they pretend, indeed, to regard the customary law as explanatory of Muslim law or as supplementary to it. This is mere fiction. Thus tribal descent goes through women—a man is a member of his mother's tribe until by marriage he is received into his wife's. Land can be owned by women only. Women may not travel; the husband settles in his wife's village—not the wife in her husband's. Exogamy is insisted on. In any conflict between customary and Muslim law the latter goes to the wall. The Malays were prepared to adopt Muslim law in purely religious matters, such as the control of mosque-lands and the levying of tithes; but when it came to the serious business of life—such as contract, sale, slave-right, land-tenure, debt and succession to titles and real property—the chiefs continued to observe their own customary law. Muslim law allows a man to dispose of one-third of his property by will. When a Malay makes a will, he does so in order to leave money to charity or to the mosque authorities as a sort of fine for having neglected his religious obligations during his life-time; he does not make a will to favour one heir at the cost of another, nor has he the power to disinherit. If all the heirs agree to an unequal distribution of the property among them-selves, they are at liberty to do so, but they are not compelled to recognize any special legacy made to one or more of them out of the available third of the estate.

The present distribution of the schools of law is as follows: *Hanafī:* Turkey, Central Asia and India. *Shāfi'ī:* Egypt, South Arabia (except the highlands of Yemen which are *Zaidī*), East Indies and East Africa. *Mālikī:* Upper Egypt, North Africa, West Africa and the French Sudan. *Ḥanbalī:* Wahhābī Arabia.

The eclipse of the Ḥanbalī school is surprising for as late as 1400 it had many scholars round the east end of the Mediter-ranean. Earlier they had been a truculent crowd, prone to violence and responsible for many riots. A Shāfi'ī author of the fifteenth century mentions them with respect.

One writer over-simplifies the situation; he says that there were two tendencies in Islam, the rigorist and the lax; the one held that everything was forbidden unless it was expressly allowed by the law, the other that everything was allowed unless it was definitely forbidden.

Khārijī

These deserve separate notice because one of the sects, the Ibāḍī, still exists in Oman and in Africa, in Mzab. Their attitude to other Muslims is best shown by their dislikes. They think 'Uthmān deserved to be killed. They condemn some of the great men of early Islam for reasons, only some of which are mentioned. They condemn:

'Alī because he ceased to fight against the rebels before his death and killed four thousand pious Companions (Khārijīs);

Ṭalḥa and Zubair because they swore fealty to 'Alī and then fought against him;

Ḥasan and Ḥusain because they supported their father, a sinner;

Mu'āwiya because he fought against 'Alī, arranged the arbitration, and shed Muslim blood;

Abū Mūsā and 'Amr because they were the arbitrators;

Yazīd because he made himself caliph and killed Ḥusain;

The Shī'a because they accept traditions as law, claim to have knowledge apart from what came through the Koran, expect a resurrection before the last day, reject the Koran, and condemn Abū Bakr and 'Umar.

The Ibāḍīs consider themselves the only true Muslims. There can be no argument about faith which does not need proof and there is no individual interpretation. A commonplace list of virtues is preceded by these; a believer must let relatives, neighbours, and wayfarers have their rights, give back deposits, act as a witness, act justly and reasonably, do right, not look at what is forbidden, lead a chaste life, and avoid lies. Further, after summoning heretics to repent, they must fight them till they return to the true faith. Lamentation for the dead, including the beating of the cheeks, is forbidden. Nowadays in Oman 'they make religion difficult', forbid music and smoking (the bedouin smoke), cut the moustache close, and do not suffer the beard to be trimmed. Chickens are unclean; this is probably a local custom and nothing to do with religion. A missionary says, "these redoubtable Ibāḍīs are ruled by their wives".

The community at Mzab is ruled by a council of divines, a relic of the council of the chief, to which in later times laymen have been added. Their law (*qānūn*) has now been written. Parallel with this though subordinate to it is a council of women, the washers of the dead, which rules the women of the community. Washing the dead is everywhere a pious act; members of the council of divines perform this service for males. The women are usually elderly with leisure enough to give themselves to the task. A few years ago the council of women was the mouthpiece of one woman who held her position by virtue of her personality. These are religious bodies but religion governs the whole of life. The sanction applied by the councils is excommunication; no one will wash the corpse of an excommunicate nor pray at his grave. The ban can only be removed by public confession and penance. Before death confession is made to a divine, even by a woman. The penances imposed may amount to one-third of the fortune and the heirs pay them exactly.

Mzab is not self-supporting so the men emigrate to earn a living but always return to the homeland; women may not emigrate. One result is that women play a large part in the life of the district; they have always been better educated than other Muslim women and, in the absence of their husbands, have to look after the family interests. "The bride price given by the law to women is the reward for the burden of pregnancy, suckling, and training which rests on her". Contrary to the general rule, marriage may be consummated before puberty. In theory a Muslim woman may marry a man from the people of the book. If a man disappears, his wife must wait four years before she can presume his death and then follows the normal period of a widow's mourning, four months and ten days. A man has also to wait four years before he can presume the death of his wife. In some ways the Khārijī conscience is very tender; if you find a fig lying under a fig tree, the correct thing is to pin the fig to the tree.

CHAPTER VI

SECTS

Shī'a

The name means 'party, followers' but, when used absolutely, it denotes a sect of Islam, being a contraction for 'the party of 'Alī'. It began as a political party among the Arabs and looked to 'Alī, the cousin and son-in-law of Muḥammad, and his descendants for leadership. Soon this movement was localized in Iraq and identified with local patriotism. The Arabs there resented being ruled from Damascus and getting a smaller share of the wealth of the state than the Arabs of Syria. Agitation led to the execution of twelve of the leading men of Kufa. When the first Umayyad caliph died, Ḥusain a son of 'Alī listened to a call from Iraq and left Medina with his family and a few followers to seek a kingdom there. He was intercepted by government troops, the Arabs of Kufa, who had invited him, stayed safely at home, so the little band of men was slain and the women and children were made prisoners. If this skirmish had been only an incident in politics it would not have been worth mentioning but it put emotion at the service of the Shī'a and became of the first importance. Today they tell you, "We hate Yazīd", the caliph at whose orders the catastrophe happened. Ḥusain has become a martyr, whom some put beside Jesus, and the tale of his sufferings fires enthusiasm for the unlucky family and inflames hatred for their oppressors. A pretended prophecy says, "Your two grandsons will fall under the blows of a despicable enemy, not because they have somehow transgressed the commands of God. Phoenix of the universe! the foulness of sin has never defiled one of your family; rather are they sacrificed for the deliverance of the nations who accept Islam, that the brows of the martyrs may reflect the whiteness of God's elect. If you desire the sins of these wicked nations to be forgiven, do not oppose the untimely plucking of these two roses from your garden".

(The two roses are Ḥusain's daughter and Ḥasan's son.)

Veneration was also felt for those companions of Muḥammad who were faithful to 'Alī. Chief of these was Salmān the Persian. He is said to have tried several religions, was sold as a slave and brought to Medina where he became a Muslim and was set free by Muḥammad. According to the Shī'a he became the confidential adviser of Muḥammad and was bequeathed by him to 'Alī in the same capacity. With a few others he was the leader in all the activities of the Shī'a, was ready to fight for 'Alī's rights and only desisted when 'Alī did homage to Abū Bakr. Also according to tradition Muḥammad declared that Salmān was one of his family and this is the foundation of his importance. "Salmān possessed the first and the second knowledge; he is the gate of God on earth; whoever accepts him, is a believer and whoever rejects him is an infidel." The extremists made him out to be a prophet; later he became the patron saint of trade guilds and his tomb is still a place of pilgrimage.

Mukhtār, who was a self-seeking adventurer, led a rebellion to avenge the death of Ḥusain but he proclaimed his allegiance to another son of 'Alī who was not a descendant of Muḥammad. His troops consisted of natives of Iraq under Arab leaders. Generation after generation descendants of Ḥusain claimed to be the head of the state but they were kept under strict supervision, often state prisoners, by the caliphs and had little influence on the history of the time. When the Umayyads had ruled a hundred years a great conspiracy was formed, secret agents were active, apocalyptic books were eagerly read, and the hopes of the Shī'a were high. But others also wanted the prize; the Abbasids ousted the Shī'a and succeeded to the Umayyads as lords of the Muslim world. The line of Shī'ite imams went on; pious writers tell of their learning, wisdom, and piety but one wonders how much of these virtues was visible to their contemporaries.

The cardinal articles of the Shī'ite creed are belief in the unity of God, in the prophets, and in the imams after them. What marks the Shī'a off from other Muslims is the doctrine of the imam for so they preferred to call the head of the state. The imam is an essential part of religion; he is chosen by God either directly or through a preceding imam; sometimes he is announced by name and sometimes only a description of him is given. God must appoint him as an act of grace so that men can perform the duties imposed by reason and avoid evil. He can make no mistake and commit no sin; he is the intermediary between God and man. 'Whoso knows not the imam of his age dies the death of a heathen.' He overshadows the prophet; the prophet may sin, the imam cannot. He is the interpreter of the word of God as written in the Koran, the guardian of the law, and the final court of appeal in all matters. The importance of the imam was enhanced by the doctrine of the 'light' of Muḥammad; this was the first thing to be created, it appeared in Adam, then in all subsequent prophets, and finally in the imam. To one who loves 'Alī and his family all sins are forgiven. As the imam is the authorized interpreter of God's will, the Koran retires into the background. In theology the Shī'a agrees generally with the Mu'tazila but the doctrine of the created Koran is passed over in silence. It is probably true that Persian ideas of legitimacy and the divinity of kings encouraged these beliefs but the party was Arab in origin. The sufferings of the imams are emphasized. 'Alī stated that he was always being wronged since his mother bore him, for his brother, when he had sore eyes, would cry, "Do not put medicinal powder in my eyes till you have put it in 'Alī's eyes". And they put it in mine though they were quite healthy. The idea was generalized into, 'Trouble falls more quickly on a pious believer than rain to the earth'.

The main body of the Shī'a recognize a succession of twelve imams the last of whom disappeared in 878. For some years after his disappearance they believed that certain men were in contact with him and made known his will to men. They await his return as the mahdī who will fill the earth with justice as it is now filled with injustice. In the meantime scholars are the religious leaders of the people. Shī'ism became the national religion of Persia in 1502 but the leading scholars have usually lived in Iraq, at Karbala where Ḥusain was killed and at Najaf where 'Alī is buried. The sect is strong in Iraq and well represented in India.

The Shī'a has much the same organization as *sunnī* Islam; it has its collections of traditions, exegesis of the Koran, system of law, and standard of life which might be called its *sunna*. In theology they teach that God can change his mind, this is a transfer of the idea of abrogation (*naskh*) from the sphere of law to that of history, they allow a man to conceal his religion if public acknowledgement of it would endanger his life. Some examples of the differences in law follow. Food prepared by Christians or Jews is not lawful, so also are eels and a vegetable which was first created from the blood of Ḥusain. Marriage with Jewish or Christian women is forbidden. Temporary marriage is allowed; a man arranges a marriage with a woman for a fixed time and pays her an agreed sum of money. When the time is up, the marriage is automatically dissolved and can only be continued by a new contract. One insignificant point of law has become the shibboleth of the sect. In certain circumstances a *sunnī* Muslim may wipe his shoes instead of washing his feet before prayer. The Shī'a does not allow this and books on theology gravely record that X did or did not permit the wiping of the shoes.

The Shī'a has its special festivals, among them the 'Pool' which commemorates Muḥammad's appointing 'Alī his successor at the pool of Khumm. The most spectacular festival is the mourning for Ḥusain which takes place during the first ten days of Muḥarram, the first month of the lunar year. During the day men parade the streets beating their backs with chains. At night processions recall the events of the fatal day. Closed litters carried by horses or camels represent the women of the party; Ḥusain's daughter had just been married so the meats for the wedding feast are carried in the procession. The villain of the piece, the man who slew Ḥusain is in red. Story has it that a Frank was so struck by the courage of the martyrs that he joined them and was slain with them. In Baghdad he has his place in the show, recognizable by European clothes, sun-helmet and umbrella. In India the tomb of Ḥusain made of bamboo and paper is part of the procession; afterwards it is thrown into the sea, burnt or buried. On the last night enthusiasts gash themselves with swords. Another form of the celebration is to have a regular miracle play acted in the courtyard of a big house.

The Shī'a make pilgrimages to their holy places in Iraq.

Arrived at the shrine, the pilgrim purifies himself by the prescribed ablutions, at the threshold asks the saint's permission to enter, circumambulates the grave thrice, and then prostrates himself twice before the tomb, all to the accompaniment of prayers and recitations and, it may be added, of gifts to the keepers of the shrine.

Religion fills the whole life and for the Shī'a religion is the imam. The reason why babies laugh and cry without apparent cause is that every infant sees and has converse with the imam; it cries when the imam is absent and laughs when he approaches it. But when the child begins to talk, this door is shut upon it and it forgets.

The strongholds of the Shī'a are Iraq, Persia and North India; the Metawila (rightly Mutawālī) of Syria are an orthodox branch accepting twelve imams.

Zaidī

This section of the Shī'a is closest to the *sunnī* Muslims. They recognized any descendant of Ḥasan or Ḥusain, the two sons of 'Alī, as imam if he could win the leadership by the sword and possessed the other qualifications of an imam. They admitted that there might be no imam and also allowed two imams at the same time if they ruled in widely separated lands. The secret designation of an imam was possible; that is to say that he must be a scholar, able to teach his people, and must claim his rights by force of arms. Zaidī imams ruled in Tabaristan, south of the Caspian sea, from 864 to 928 and in Yemen another founded a state in 893 which has lasted with interruptions till the present day. At first the capital was Sa'da but San'a was captured in 1591 and became the capital. Naturally many of the imams have been scholars and have written much, especially on law. One of the oldest law books is a Zaidī code. The Zaidīs are confined to the highlands and the lowlands have always been *sunnī*.

They do not call the first three caliphs usurpers and refrain from cursing them. They are Mu'tazilī in theology, severe in their ethical code, and averse from mysticism; no dervish orders are allowed in Yemen today, They follow the Shī'a in adding the words, "come to the best of work" to the call to prayer; in not allowing the 'wiping of the shoes'; and in regarding the flesh of animals slaughtered by non-Muslims as unclean. They differ from them in not permitting temporary marriage. They agree with the Khawārij in calling wicked Muslims unbelievers. The many Jews in Yemen do not carry arms and it is more disgraceful for a Muslim to kill a Jew than to kill a woman.

Ismā'īlīs

Those who acknowledge twelve imams say that Ja'far the sixth intended to appoint his eldest son Ismā'īl as his successor but found that he was a drunkard and so passed him over in favour of another son; they also assert that Ismā'īl died before his father. Some, however, refused to credit his death, affirmed that his father had appointed him imam, and that the appointment once made could not be rescinded. These were called Ismā'īlīs or Seveners; other names are Bāṭinī (esoteric) because they held that all the facts of religion had an allegorical sense and Ta'līmī (instructionist) because the imam alone could teach the true religion.

Nothing is known about the early history of the sect. At the end of the ninth century it was firmly established and in 969 an Ismā'īlī dynasty, the Fatimids, ruled in Egypt. In 1021 the first secession took place when the Druzes refused to believe that the caliph Ḥākim had died and regarded him as God. In 1094 a more serious breach occurred; at the death of Mustanṣir his younger son Musta'lī seized power, displacing the elder son, Nistār; the best known representatives of this branch were the Assassins; the Aga Khan is the present head of this branch. After the fall of the Fatimid dynasty Yemen became the centre of the Musta'lī branch; from there it spread to India where a schism occurred, into the Sulaimānīs, a small sect, and the Dāūdīs or Bōhorās.

Belief. Neo-Platonism is the basis of the system. Nothing can be said about God because any such statement involves a comparison of Him with something else and 'nothing is like Him'. He is God of the two opposites, Creator of the two opponents, Judge of the two contraries. The statements that He is all-knowing and all-powerful mean that He gives power and knowledge. By means of something which is symbolized by the creative word 'be' He produced the two worlds; the inner consisting of realities, intelligences and spirits; and the outer containing the lower and higher bodies, those of the spheres and elements. The greatest body is the Throne and the next is the Footstool. Immediately below God is the universal intelligence, below that is the universal soul, below it are other emanations which govern the spheres, and the lowest of all is the active intelligence which controls the present world. The universal soul is imperfect and yearns for union with the perfection of the universal intelligence; this yearning produces the circular movement of the spheres. Both worlds move from perfection to imperfection and back again till they both end in the command which is the word 'be' and escape from the chain of living of which the beginning and end is God.

Man differs from the rest of the universe because he is fit to receive the divine light. The universal intelligence is represented among men by a series of seven prophets or speakers, Adam, Noah, Abraham, Moses, Jesus, Muḥammad, and Ismā'īl. Each was accompanied by a representative of the world soul—a silent one or base. Moses had Aaron, Jesus had Peter, and Muḥammad had 'Alī.' The prophet judges the external world; his law is twofold, external and revealed, interpreted and internal. The imam is the manifestation of the divine command and is accompanied by his 'argument' who is the manifestation of the universal soul. The argument gets supernatural knowledge from the imam and is the teacher of men. What the universal intelligence is to the universe that is the imam to the world of men; without him it could not be. He judges the internal world and interprets the law of the prophet. "God must set up an imam to teach men the knowledge of God and guide them to the proofs and purposes." First came prophets, then visible imams, and then the hidden imams; when the imam is visible, his messengers are hidden, when he is concealed, his messengers are visible. Codes of law are spiritual worlds and worlds are materialized laws. The end will be when the soul reaches perfection by rising to the universal intelligence by the virtue of the imam and to union with it; the earth will be changed, the heavens folded like a paper, good will be separated from evil, all partial good will be united with the universal soul and all partial evil with the devil.

It is commonly said that the Ismā'īlī movement was a conspiracy to destroy religion, that there were seven or nine grades of initiation and, while the lower grades were allowed to keep their rites and beliefs, the higher cast off all religion. It is claimed that these charges are libels. The Ismā'īlīs insisted on the strict observance of all religious duties for there can be no internal without an external. In their earliest literature no mention is made of initiation; the belief that it existed may be due to the fact that instruction was adapted to the capacity of the pupil. The later Nistārī branch paid more attention to the inward aspects of the teaching than did the Fatimids; this was the new teaching associated with the lords of Alamut. The system of law is very like that of the Shī'a.

The Fatimid caliphs claimed to be the descendants of 'Alī; their opponents denied that claim flatly. This is not the place to examine the evidence. Certain ideas occur again and again; the internal and external, the speaker and the silent, the servant entrusted with a deposit and the young heir who is not yet ready to receive it. It has been suggested that in the Fatimid genealogy there are two series of imams, the legitimate and the functional who had the task of preserving the sacred knowledge till he, who should use it, should come.

Qarmaṭī

This is probably a nickname given by their enemies. This sect was closely connected with the Ismā'īlīs but the exact relationship is uncertain. Ḥamdān Qarmaṭ began to preach on the borders of Iraq and Persia about 890 giving himself out to be the agent of some great one. He established a base which he called the House of Emigration. He levied taxes, alms at the breaking of the fast, dues for the use of the House of Emigration, a fifth of all property, and dues for partaking of a communion meal; he introduced communism in the necessaries of life. From 890 till 990 they terrorized Iraq, Syria and North Arabia; one branch founded a state in Ḥasa which lasted from 894 till 1030. The men of this state captured Mecca in 930 and carried off the Black Stone; it was only returned in 950 at the command of the Fatimid caliph. Usually the Qarmaṭīs obeyed the orders of the Fatimid caliphs though, once at least, they fought against them; for reasons of policy the Fatimids found it convenient at times to disown their turbulent servants. The state in Ḥasa was founded by Abū Sa'īd and then was ruled by a council of six of his descendants, helped by six ministers. They accepted Muḥammad as a prophet, had no mosque and expected the return of Abū Sa'īd; they observed neither the daily prayers nor the fast. Something like State socialism existed; the Government owned thirty thousand slaves who were employed in the fields and gardens. The inhabitants paid only the land tax. If a man fell into debt or could not keep his house in repair, the Government advanced him the money. If a poor stranger arrived, money was lent to him to buy tools and keep himself till he could earn his own living. Inside the state leaden money was used and it might not be exported.

Nuṣairī

They live in Northern Syria, largely in the sanjak of Alexandretta, and in Cilicia. There are two worlds, of light and darkness, each being sevenfold. There have been seven cycles of history in each of which the deity, which has no attributes and is beyond comprehension, manifested itself. The highest manifestation is the Meaning. That from the light of its own essence created the Name; this is the abode of the Meaning, the veil behind which it hides itself, and the moment of manifestation of the hidden divine. The name created from the glow of its light the Gate which is the vehicle of manifestation. These three are closely connected but are not equal; "I turn to the Gate; I bow before the Name, I adore the Meaning". In this last cycle the Meaning is 'Alī, who is recognized outwardly as imam but inwardly as God, this being an attempt to bridge the gap between the absolute and the world; the Name is Muḥammad, and the Gate is Salmān. Salmān created the five Incomparables who rule respectively thunder and earthquakes, the stars, the winds and the death of men, human bodies and sicknesses, and the entry of men's spirits into their bodies. These five created the world of darkness.

Nuṣairīs were at first stars in the world of light but fell through disobedience; light descends into the darkness to bring the souls, which are shut up in bodies as in prisons, back to the light; after seven transmigrations the pious will return to the world of light. Women have no part in religion.

No building is set apart for worship. A youth has to be initiated into the secrets of the religion, a process consisting of three stages. The first is a solemn oath not to reveal anything of the spiritual marriage whereby the word of the initiator fertilizes the soul of the novice. The doctrine is the allegorical interpretation of the pillars of Islam; thus fasting is the secret preserved in the names of thirty men and thirty women, the days and nights of Ramaḍān. The Incomparables are identified with five companions of Muḥammad. They have their own festivals over and above those common to the Shī'ites and abstain from certain foods, camels, hares, and eels; crabs, gazelles, porcupines, lady's fingers, and tomatoes are forbidden to some.

Above the initiates are the shaikhs; they must belong to families of shaikhs and have spent six months in further instruction after initiation. This religion has been called gnosticism with Muslim veneer and terminology.

Druze

The Druzes are an offshoot of the Ismā'īlī sect. They believe that the Fatimid caliph Ḥākim (disappeared 1021) represented God in His unity; his eccentricities and cruelties are explained symbolically; he was the last incarnation of God and is not dead but in a state of occultation. Below him are five superior ministers, incarnations of emanations from deity; They are the *ḥudūd* (bounds, precepts). They are: the universal reason; the universal soul; the word which was produced by reason from the soul; the right wing or preceder; the left wing or follower. At the time of Ḥākim these were incarnate in five men. There are three classes of lower rank which are not incarnations; they are *dā'ī* (preacher) or industry; *Ma'dhūn* (permitted) or opening; and *mukassir* (destroyer), *naqīb* (overseer), or phantom.

There are seven moral rules. The Druzes must love truth; this only applies among themselves. If a Druze tells a falsehood to those of another faith, he must take the first opportunity of telling a co-religionist, who has heard it, that it is a falsehood. They must watch over each other's safety. They must renounce the religion to which they formerly belonged. They must avoid the devil and all living in error. They must recognize in all ages the principles of divine unity in humanity. They must be satisfied with the acts of 'Our Lord" Ḥākim, whatever they are. They must be resigned to his will (? as manifested through his ministers).

The Druzes are divided into initiates (*'āqil*) and the ignorant (*jāhil*); initiates only meet in the place of worship, the *khalwa*, on Thursday evenings, the beginning of Friday according to eastern reckoning. The most meritorious of the initiates, about one in fifty, become perfect (*ajwad*). Metempsychosis is an accepted doctrine. It is commonly said that the number of the sect is constant; there are Druzes in China, if one dies there, one is born in Syria and vice versa.

Bektashī

This order of dervishes was in existence at the beginning of the sixteenth century; it is certain that it was not founded by Ḥajjī Bektash, probably there was no such person. The ideas behind the order are older and more widely spread; the Kizil-Bash in eastern Asia Minor and the Ahl-i-Ḥaqq in Persia agree in their main doctrines with the Bektashīs though they lack the rigid organization of the order. Mystical ideas of the original equality of all religions and the worthlessness of ritual forms prevail. Christian, gnostic, and pagan elements have been incorporated. Usually the Bektashīs profess to be *sunnī* but they are extreme Shī'ites; they recognize the twelve imams, particularly Ja'far and revere fourteen Shī'ite martyrs. Bektashīs have often settled at old places of pilgrimage and so appropriated them for the order. Prayers at saints' tombs may replace the ritual worship, the Muslim prayers. They have a trinity, God, Muḥammad, 'Alī; celebrate a sort of communion with bread, wine, and cheese; confess their sins to their chiefs, and receive absolution. Wine is not forbidden and their women are not veiled. They have adopted a mystic theory of numbers and believe in transmigration of souls. There are no outstanding peculiarities in the organization. One section is celibate and has a head of its own who lives at the mother monastery. Their political importance was due to the connection of the order with the Janissaries and it was concerned in many Janissary revolts. Many of its monasteries were destroyed when the Janissaries were suppressed. The cap of the order is made of twelve wedge-shaped pieces of cloth, to symbolize the twelve imams; in full dress the double axe is carried.

Kizil-Bash

'Red heads', among other meanings, is the name given to a sect in Turkey which calls itself 'Alawī and is clearly connected with the Nuṣairī. For them 'Alī is an incarnation of God as had been Jesus and others before him. God is one in three persons; below Him are five archangels, twelve ministers, and forty saints. The Virgin Mary is revered and litanies sung in her honour. In a service at night-time the officiating priest sings prayers in honour of 'Alī, Jesus, Moses and David; he holds in his hand a willow wand which he dips in water; this water is then distributed among the homes. After confession of sins the priest imposes penance. The lights are put out and the congregation laments its sins. The lights are lit again the priest pronounces the absolution (it may be delayed) and a communion service follows. These people do not observe Muslim ablutions and prayers, do not fast during Ramaḍān; they drink wine, but fast during the first twelve days of Muḥarram, lamenting Ḥasan and Ḥusain. They do not shave the head and let the beard grow. At the head of the sect are two patriarchs who are regarded as descendants of 'Alī and are invested with divine power. Lower in the hierarchy are bishops and priests.

Ahl-i-Ḥaqq

These used to be called 'Alī-ilāhī but the name is not suitable because 'Alī is not the central figure in the faith. They live in Western Persia; religiously they are not a unity but a congeries of subjects with ideas ranging from the primitive to the pseudo-philosophical. They believe in seven successive manifestations of deity; these are compared to garments which it puts on. Each is accompanied by four (or five) angels who are emanations of deity. The deity was at first enclosed in a pearl; it showed itself first in the creator of the world then in 'Alī, and later in Sulṭān Ṣohāk who is regarded as the founder of the religion. The angels accompanying any manifestation are incarnations of their predecessors and may be called by their names. They also believe in the transmigration of souls, "Fear not the punishment of death; the death of a man is like a duck's diving under water". Man has to pass through one thousand and one incarnations in which he receives the reward of his actions; another version says that men are naturally good or bad according to the colour of the clay from which they were made. The coming of the 'Lord of the ages' is desired who will "fulfil the wishes of his friends and encompass the universe".

Worship takes the form of meetings where sacred texts are recited to music; on great occasions, which are called *dhikr*, dervishes excited to ecstasy by music tread on live coals or take them in their hands. Offerings, prepared food or animals, are an essential part of these meetings; the animals are killed, the bones buried, and the flesh divided among the assistants. As in the dervish orders, every member must have a teacher (*pīr*); attachment to a teacher serves as initiation and is regarded as a blood bond so that the novice cannot marry into the family of his teacher. A union between one man (or several) and a woman is arranged 'for moral perfection' and with a view to the resurrection. A like usage is found among the Yazīdīs. Fasting is strict but lasts only three days; it takes place in winter and is followed by a festival.

The religion is eclectic with doctrines of the extreme Shī'a as a foundation; they have twelve imams but 'Alī is not the central figure. The likeness to the dervish orders is obvious. 'God in a pearl' and the purification of the men of light by their transmigrations are Manichaean.

Ḥurūfī

The Ḥurūfī sect was founded at the end of the fourteenth century by Faḍlullāh of Asterabad. He seems to have taken his ideas from the Ismā'īlīs. The world is eternal and always in circular motion; this movement is the cause of all change. Change goes in cycles; each begins with an Adam and ends with a judgement. God reveals Himself in man, especially in his face. Revelation is in three stages, prophecy, holiness, and deity. Muḥammad was the last of the prophets; the imams from 'Alī to Ḥasan 'Askarī were the saints, while Faḍlullāh was the last of the saints and the first of the divine series, God become flesh. The sect got its name from its fancies about letters and numbers, fancies which were borrowed by the Bektashīs. Unlike the dervish order, the Ḥurūfīs had no special ritual but practised a form of communion with wine, bread, and cheese.

Khōja.

The name of a sect which is found mainly in the Punjab, Sindh, the Bombay Presidency, in Zanzibar and its neighbourhood, and under the name Mawālī or Mawlāī on the north-west frontier of India and in scattered groups in Central Asia. In India they are descendants of converts and in Zanzibar immigrants from India. The Bombay section and its dependencies regards the sacred person of the Aga Khan as the head of the community and pays to him tithe and dues at births, marriages, burials and the new moon; but each congregation is otherwise independent, having its own centre which is meeting-house and mosque, and its own officials, president, treasurer and secretary. These are sometimes appointed by the Aga Khan but are usually elected. The Ismā'īlī teaching was adapted to the Hindus; thus it is stated in the *Das-Avatār* that the tenth incarnation of Vishnu (which Hindus expect in the future) took place in the person of 'Alī or in the unrevealed imam. A Persian book written about 1594 for the instruction of the Indian Khōjas is revered in its old Sindhi form as the twenty-sixth in the list of Khōja saints.

The Muslim law of succession does not apply to them; till recently their marriages were performed before a *sunnī* judge; no divorce is permitted without the sanction of the community which usually requires the consent of both parties; a second wife is not allowed during the lifetime of the first without the approval of the community which is usually granted if two thousand rupees are deposited for the support of the first wife. When death approaches, water is sprinkled to the reading of the *Das-Avatār*.

The Khōjas in Central Asia belong to the Nistārī branch of the Ismā'īlīs. Those in the Punjab do not recognize the Aga Khan as head but go to *sunnī* members of the Qādirī or Chishtī orders for religious guidance. Originally the beliefs of the Bombay branch were the same as those of the Punjab group but respect for the Aga Khan has removed them from the influence of the Indian religious orders.

There is unrest in the sect. In 1927 the Khōja Reformers' Society addressed these demands to the Aga Khan:

> "That you will disclaim and repudiate all divine honours paid to you which belong rightly only to the true God Almighty.
>
> That you will change commercial Jama'at Khanas (meeting-houses) into mosques where prayer only might be offered. That you will arrange for Islamic instruction being imparted to one and all of the followers of Your Highness. That you will absolutely stop and refuse acceptance of all offerings whatsoever, pecuniary or kind; and lastly, That you will be good enough to abolish the councils and repeal the rules altogether, for we respectfully point out that this is the right of the community as an autonomous body, which alone is competent to govern itself and manage its own affairs."

Bōhorā, Bōhrā, Bahūrā.

They are mostly descendants of converted Hindus in the Bombay Presidency belonging for the most part to the Musta'lī division of the Ismā'īlīs. The name means trader; the majority are traders and Ismā'īlī while the minority are peasants and *sunnī*. The Ja'farī Bōhrās also are *sunnī*. The conversions began in the eleventh or twelfth century. After the fall of the Fatimid dynasty the head of the sect fled from Egypt to Yemen and the Bōhrās went on pilgrimage to him there, paid him the tithe, and took their disputes to him for settlement till in 1539 he removed to India. In 1588 those in Yemen did not recognize the Indian choice of Dāūd as head of the sect and set up Sulaimān, thus starting a schism. The head of the Sulaimānī branch lived in Yemen but had a deputy in India; this branch is now few in number. The head (*mullā* or *dā'ī*) of the Dāūdī branch has lived in Surat since the middle of the eighteenth century. He is the supreme authority in religious and legal affairs; discipline is maintained by fines and serious offences are punished by expulsion from the sect. They are said to pay one-fifth of their income to the *mullā* and further dues on births, marriages and funerals. They keep the tenets of their faith secret. They have their own mosques and cemeteries, observe only three prayers daily, and do not keep the special Friday prayer. They light illuminations on the Hindu festival of Diwālī and begin new account books on that day.

Momna. The Momnas or Memons of Cutch are Shī'a in name but they do not associate with Muslims, eat no flesh, reverence the cow, are not circumcised, do not observe the five daily prayers nor the fast of Ramaḍān. Their salutation is Rām, Rām; they worship the Hindu triad and consider Imām Shāh, the missionary who originally converted them about three hundred years ago, an incarnation of Brahmā.

Wahhābī

Although modern in date this movement is not modern in outlook. In the middle of the eighteenth century Muḥammad ibn 'Abd al-Wahhāb was moved by his study of the works of Ibn Taimiya to become a follower of Ibn Ḥanbal and protest against the innovations which had invaded Islam. Strong in the support of his son-in-law Ibn Sa'ūd, a chief of Najd, the movement swept through Arabia and is now the religion of all the peninsula except the south. Every revolution has claimed to be a return to the Koran and this one is no exception but it meant what it said. They call themselves Unitarians or Muslims; it is only their adversaries who call them Wahhābīs. There is no intermediary between God and man so they abominate the worship of saints and condemn prayers and sacrifices to them as idolatry; when they captured Mecca in 1806 they destroyed the tombs which others venerated. Quite as much as the Khārijīs they deserve to be called the Puritans of Islam. When possible, all prayers should be said in the mosque which is very plain. Simplicity in dress is essential, gold ornaments are forbidden, and there is no music. The sect has encouraged the legalistic spirit against which Ghazālī protested; in answer to a question one of them said after long consideration that the first sin was idolatry but he declared without any hesitation that the second was tobacco. The devil micturated on a field and the resultant crop was tobacco.

The following list contains the main ideas of the sect. God is the only object of worship and whose who worship any other deserve death. Most men are not monotheists because they try to win God's favour by visiting the graves of saints. They are like the idolaters of Mecca spoken of in the Koran. It is polytheism to mention the name of a prophet, saint or angel in prayer, to ask the intercession of anyone with God or to make vows to any but Him. It is unbelief to accept as knowledge anything that is not confirmed by the Koran, *sunna* or strict reasoning. It is unbelief and heresy to deny God's control of all acts. It is unbelief to employ allegorical interpretation of the Koran. Wahhābī teaching differs from that of Ibn Ḥanbal in that it makes attendance at prayer in public a duty; the shaving of the beard and the use of abusive language are punished by the judge at his discretion; religious alms are paid on the profits of trade and not only on visible capital; the utterance of the confession does not make a man a Muslim so that an animal killed by such a man is not lawful food for a Muslim.

A traveller writes: There are no eating houses in Wahhābī land. An honourable man cannot go to a place where he pays for what he eats and others see him. When the looker-on is hungry and has no money to buy, the eater is ashamed and the looker-on filled with forbidden desires. Houses and clothes are plain, laughter and music are forbidden and singing is effeminate. Chess is forbidden because it might make the players forget the hour of prayer.

As to moral value there are not five classes of acts but three only, the commanded, the forbidden, and the indifferent.

CHAPTER VII

MYSTICISM

Muḥammad began his mission as a preacher of the judgement, the day of the Lord was at hand and it behoved all men to repent; often he used the argument that the joys of this world are as nothing compared to the bliss or misery of eternity. This side of his teaching was neglected when the judgement was delayed and energies were absorbed in the conquests. Still there were a faithful few who fixed their eyes on the hereafter and scorned the goods of this world. It is worthy of note that one word used to describe the religious life originally meant 'to be dirty'. Among the signs of religion were: poverty and its counterpart, trust in God. One convinced of the futility of this world had no need for wealth. A man was offered money but refused it, saying, "I have a goat to give us milk and a beast to ride; what more do I want?" It is God who gives man his food, so a store of provisions was felt to be a lack of trust in Him. Some would not have more than a day's food in the house, others not more than enough for the next meal. One never bought himself a shirt and could not sleep if he had money in the house for he said, "If a man keeps money in the house overnight and does not know what God will send him, he has had no experience of Him". They are fond of repeating that, when Muḥammad died, his coat of mail was in pawn to a Jew.

Celibacy. Muḥammad had set his face against celibacy but a few of his followers practised it. One quotation is enough, "I am eighty-four and nothing is more terrible to me than women."

Fasting. Many went beyond keeping the fast of Ramaḍān; Tuesday and Thursday were favourite days for fasting. Some fasted continuously. It was not unusual to take a vow to perform the pilgrimage without speaking. Of course, there were protests against excess of any sort. A bedouin asked, "Shall I let loose my camel and trust in God?" He got the answer, "Tie up your camel and trust in God". If any one fasted overmuch, he became too weak to perform the daily prayers, a nobler work than fasting, and even less able to join in the holy war.

Seriousness. The thought of the judgement lay heavy on these men so life was earnest. One was always sad 'as if he were coming from the funeral of a dear friend'. They said of another that, if fire were mentioned, he looked as if it had been created only for him. One would not give his little daughter leave to play; he could not bring himself to utter such a frivolous word. Much weeping was a sign of this frame of mind; one lost his sight thereby.

Prayer. Fear of the judgement kept the thought of God ever before these men. Muḥammad had spoken often of the profit to be got from prayer at night so it became the rule for the devout to spend hours of the dark in prayer.

Imagination has run riot in picturing these men. Salmān the Persian was governor of Medāïn; he had no house but sat under a tree following the shade as it moved round and earned his living by weaving mats. Another got his living by gathering date stones. 'Alī is made out to be the model religious; he so felt the cold that his limbs trembled yet he would not accept money from the treasury to buy warm clothes; he wore short garments, ate coarse food, slept little, prayed long at night, and practised self-examination. The last item is a flagrant anachronism.

With Ḥasan of Basra insight into religion is deeper as is shown by the following sayings which may well be genuine:

> We have met men who were more chary of taking what God allowed them than of taking what He had forbidden.
>
> The world is your horse, if you ride it, it carries you; but if it rides you, it will kill you.
>
> A little temptation is from the devil but a persistent temptation is from desire; fasting, prayer, and self-discipline will help you to master it.
>
> We never knew anyone who followed after the world and obtained heaven; the reverse is true.

The next stage was to stress the motive for the religious life, love to God. This stage is summed up in the sentence, "I have not served God from fear of hell for I should be a wretched hireling if I served Him from fear; nor from love of heaven for I should be a bad servant if I served for what was given; I have served Him only for love of Him and desire for Him". This concentration on God left no room in the heart for anything else. A man explained that he fondled his child because he loved him and was rebuked for the love of God should be strong enough to exclude mere human affections. The critic still had a long way to go in the religious life! Other expressions of the idea are, "I love the apostle of God dearly but love of the Creator has turned me aside from love of His creatures"; and, "My love for God leaves no room for hating Satan".

The temper of the mystics can be best shown by a few typical sayings:

> The most useful sin is that which you keep ever before your eyes, weep over it till death comes, and do not fall again into any like it; this is true repentance. The most harmful good deed is one which makes you forget your sins, deceives you into not fearing offences, and makes you conceited.
>
> An empty stomach with a contented heart, continuous poverty with present ascetism, and perfect patience with constant remembrance of God.
>
> We did not derive our knowledge of God from discussion, but from fasting, the renunciation of this world, and the abandonment of that to which we were accustomed and which is reckoned to be good.
>
> May God make you a student of tradition who is a mystic, not a mystic who is a student of tradition. (The basis of the mystic life is the practice of religious duties.)
>
> One moment in this world is better than a thousand years in the next, for this is the place of service and that is the place of nearness to God and nearness to Him is gained by service.
>
> O God, whatever punishment Thou dost inflict upon me, punish me not with the humiliation of being veiled fromThee.
>
> We count all torments more desirable than that of being veiled from Thee, for when Thy beauty is revealed in our hearts, we reckon tribulation as nought.

> Men hold three things dear and so bring themselves to nought; the self and they make that a god; ease and they make that a god; wealth and they make that a god. Two things men seek after and do not find, joy and rest, for both of these belong to paradise.
>
> One day I looked upon a light and I did not cease to contemplate it until I became that light.
>
> For thirty years God spoke by the tongue of Junaid and Junaid was not there and men knew it not.
>
> One refused to say, 'There is no god but God', lest he should be taken in the denial before reaching the affirmation.

The more outrageous utterances of this sort were called *shaṭḥ* and have been defined by a modern scholar as the secret movement of thought when ecstasy is so strong that the mystic cannot retain it within himself; it reveals suddenly to the solitary soul the supernatural visitation of a transcendent voice. Mystics are agreed that it results from prevenient grace and is the sign of complete purification of the soul. Some consider this passing phase to be a halting point on the path to the final dissolution of personality in the divine silence. Others believe that these contacts with the divine change the weak voice of the lover, granting him occasionally the power to take part in the dialogue between God and the self which is the talk of lovers. As examples may be quoted: "My intercession is more efficacious than Muḥammad's. Thou obeyest me more than I obey Thee. Adam sold his God for a scrap of food. Thy paradise is a child's game." "Leader of those who go astray, lead me astray, further, further." "To perfect lovers prayer is atheism." "I am two years younger than my Lord."

One writer calls such sayings exaggerated and involuntary speech in a state of ecstasy for which the speaker is not responsible. They are not to be accepted as true for only prophets are infallible whereas others may fall into error, but they are not to be rejected because they are the words of gnostics who may see what is hidden from common men. It is best to keep an open mind. Another is more favourable: there is a flavour of madness about such words but what they claim is true for they come from those who speak plainly out of their knowledge but without divine permission.

The love for God, which filled the mystic, led inevitably to the idea of union with Him, either by the indwelling of God in the man or by his ascent to God. Theologians used *tawḥīd* (unification) to denote belief in one God as opposed to the unpardonable sin of worshipping more than one. The mystics put another meaning into the word; to them it meant unification with God, the sinking of the self and the abnegation of the individual will in the will of God. The true mystic was he who had cast off self and lost himself in God. By the year 800 images taken from drunkenness and sexual love were freely used to describe this experience. Here, as elsewhere mysticism became a sort of pantheism; God is the only reality and men spoke as possessed by God, "I went from God to God until they cried from me in me, saying, 'Oh thou I'," and, "For thirty years God was my mirror, now I am my own mirror". Some declared, "I am the *ḥaqq*". *Ḥaqq* cannot be translated because it means truth, right, and reality; in fact several aspects of God.

From another aspect, mysticism was the natural reaction of those repelled by the formalism of Muslim worship and by the law which judged external actions only: it therefore emphasized the springs of action. At this stage there is no rejection of the law, rather meticulous care in keeping it. There was opposition; the Shī'a condemned it because it did away with the necessity for an imam by insisting on the direct relation between God and man; the Mu'tazila condemned it because love between man and God involved likeness between them and 'nothing is like Him'. Disciples of Ibn Ḥanbal called mystics free-thinkers but the average Muslim saw nothing wrong in this way of life. It was not till 854 that a mystic came into conflict with authority and in 922 Ḥallāj was executed in Baghdad. He took over the idea of the union of the soul with God and made a theory to explain it. The essence of God's essence is love; at first He loved Himself and through love revealed Himself to Himself. Then, desiring to see that love as an external object He created Adam, an image of Himself with all His attributes. But this human nature is different from the divine; though mystically united they are not identical; personality survives even in union,

> I am he whom I love and He whom I love is I,
> We are two spirits dwelling in one body.
> If thou seest me, thou seest Him;
> And if thou seest Him, thou seest us both.

Absorption of the soul in God is the more common idea, "We are the spirit of one though we dwell by turns in two bodies", and

> Happy the moment when we are seated in the palace, thou and I,
> With two forms and two figures but with one soul, thou and I.

A suitable philosophy was at hand to express these ideas, neo-Platonism with its theory of emanations. The first, the universal intelligence, is identified with the light of Muḥammad to which God said, "I have created nothing fairer than thee". It is the duty of the mystic to work backwards along the line of emanations, to strip himself of the limitations of the body and desire, to rise superior to all external aids by the counsel of his spiritual director, and to enter into direct communion with God. The familiar metaphors recur; the world is a prison, the stages of the universe are veils to hide God, the start of the ascent is a birth, and the teacher is the spiritual father.

The spiritual life has often been described as a journey and the maps of the road are many. One gives seven stages or stations: 1. repentance, 2. abstinence, 3. renunciation, 4. poverty, 5. patience, 6. trust in God, 7. satisfaction. Only when the pilgrim has passed all the stages is he permanently raised to the higher planes of consciousness called gnosis, the truth, and realizes that knowledge, knower, and known are one. The following aphorisms are notes to the chart. Repentance means abandoning the sins of which man is conscious and resolving never to return to them. The novice may think with remorse of his sins while the adept may forget his because the thought of them comes between him and God. Poverty means being stripped of every wish that can turn man's thoughts away from God. Dying to self, which is the result of this poverty, is living to God. Here are notes to another chart. Common men repent of sins, the elect repent of inattention, and prophets repent of seeing their inability to attain what others have attained. When the mystic sees how contemptible the world is, he abstains from his abstinence from it because it is so mean. Faith is the glory of the believer, understanding is the glory of faith, patience is the glory of understanding. The poor should have no desire; but if this is impossible, he should not desire more than a bare sufficiency. Gratitude is losing sight of the gift in the giver. Fear is male, hope is female; from them are born the realities of faith. Fear and hope are as the wings of a bird; if they are equal, it can fly. God has given to those who fear all the gifts which he has given separately to other believers. Piety and conviction are the two pans of a balance and trust is the pointer which shows increase or decrease.

The end of the path is *fanā*, extinction, which has three senses:

1. A moral transformation of the soul through the extinction of all passions and desires.
2. Abstraction from all objects of perception, thoughts, actions, and feelings through concentration on the thought of God, i.e. contemplation of the divine attributes.
3. The cessation of conscious thought.

Upon this follows *baqā*, abiding in God. This also is in three stages:

1. Union with one of the activities symbolized by the names of God.
2. Union with one of the attributes of God.
3. Union with the divine essence.

In addition to the stages or stations on the path of the spirit are states; but the division between the two is not sharp. Stages are more or less permanent, states are transitory; stages are in part the result of human endeavour, states are the gift of God. Each stage has its corresponding states and progress from one stage to another is marked by the increasing frequency of states which belong to the stage above. It is tempting to say that a stage is a state become permanent.

When the mystic has reached his goal, the veils of flesh and the will have been rent asunder, truth is clearly seen, the last secret has been wrung from existence, and man is united to God. The wisest teachers admit that there is no place for words here; the knowledge that comes direct from God, cannot be communicated. Words can only suggest the ineffable. Unfortunately, many Muslim mystics ignored this limitation, strained all the resources of speech, and did violence to it in the attempt to pass on their experiences. The result is that much of mystic literature can only be called nonsense.

In the seventeenth century it was taught that only the very greatest saints could hope for union with God; the average saint had to be content with union with Muḥammad.

The usual name for a mystic is *ṣūfi*; it is almost certainly derived from the name for 'wool' and is due to the early ascetics wearing wool in imitation of the monks. Wherever Arabic is spoken a teacher is a necessity, "It is better to go wrong with a teacher than to go right by yourself". The mystics had no difficulty in following custom. Before 800 a teacher had gathered a band of disciples round him in Abbadan. In the next century houses belonging to religious communities existed. The great orders of mystics, commonly called the dervishes, were not founded till centuries later, the Qādiri order about 1200. A religious genius gathered disciples and founded a monastery (*ẓāwiya*, *tekke*), the founder was succeeded by a son or a favourite disciple, missionaries were sent out and daughter houses started. Lay brethren gathered round each house and their contributions were a regular income. The branch houses paid tribute to the original establishment. The founder gathered the odour of sanctity which was imparted in greater or less degree to his successors. The monastery might become a place of pilgrimage to receive the offerings of the faithful. Then it often happened that the branch houses lost touch and became independent orders or an enterprising brother broke away and founded an order of his own. Each order had its own dress and ritual. The general principles were the same in all.

The orders usually have something distinctive about their dress, the Mevlevīs, for instance, wear a long hat of rough felt which looks like the finger of a giant's glove.

The entrant has to pass through a novitiate before he becomes a full member and receives the cloak (*khirqa*) which is the mark of the mystic. An historian dismisses a man with the curt, "his cloak was the only thing about him which belonged to his order". Each order had its own ritual (*dhikr*); this generally consisted of a short phrase repeated interminably. Such a phrase is, *yā hū* ("oh he"; *He* refers to God), and the repetition may be accompanied with certain breathing exercises. The ritual of the Mevlevīs is the dance while *'Isāwī* dervishes gash themselves with knives or eat snakes or scorpions. Whatever form the ritual takes, the object is the same—to produce a state of ecstasy in which communion with God is easier. The order has a spiritual genealogy, as a rule, going back to a Companion; this legitimates the claim to possess religious virtue above that of ordinary men. Such a genealogy has been known to go back to Adam. Apart from worship the aims of the orders have been varied. The Senussī (founded 1837) had political aims while others were peacefully missionary and civilizing. The monastery included a school and offered food and lodging to the wayfarer. In Africa it was a centre of civilization.

A modern opinion from Morocco gives the orthodox view of the dervish orders. They were formed in the sixteenth century. Men gave their affection and veneration to one shaikh, devoting themselves to his service and exalting him above all others. They call themselves his servants, invoke his aid and turn to him in all difficulties. This way of thinking has degenerated into fanaticism and the community is divided against itself. Religious men who have special gifts, i.e. saints, are all equal like the teeth of a comb; the believer loves them in God and for God and by their aid asks help from God. The orders have their own meetings where the noise of musical instruments mingles with song, dance and heavy breathing. Sometimes fires are lighted by tricks and acclaimed as miracles. The members are so absorbed in their performance that they forget one prayer-time and even two. These meetings are even held in the mosque for they erect mosques in their convents, turn them into asylums and hold annual fairs with sacrifices. These men are really possessed by the devil but they call their madness a 'state' like the saintly mystics.

The wandering dervish, who lives on the credulity of the simple, while indulging in alcohol or drugs, is an evil parody of the true mystic.

The orders are widespread and flourishing though, of course, they have their vicissitudes; it is common for men to belong to two or three. Many men follow their trade or profession and attend the meetings of the order as a Christian might attend a weekly prayer meeting. It is obvious that the orders fill a place in the religious life of the community; a convert to Christianity said that he missed the ritual of his order and the church offered him nothing to take its place. Here follow short accounts of a few selected orders.

The Qādirī order. 'Abd al-Qādir al-Jilānī (†1166) was head of a Ḥanbalī school and of a convent in Baghdad. The collection of rules and doctrines which rested on his authority was sufficient to form a system and an order. It seems that at first the organization was lax and later the several convents differed widely in their practice. In North Africa the order is known as Jilālī; there the head of a convent names his successor but, if he fails to do so, there is an election the result of which is always confirmed by the supreme head in Baghdad. The convents are self-governing and the connection with Baghdad very loose. The headship of the convents is not hereditary. Some regard 'Abd al-Qādir as a saint and miracle worker, others regard him as the lord of creation under God while more moderate men say that this was only during his lifetime.

The Shādhilī order. This was founded about 1250 with the aim of producing a religious life. It had no buildings and the brethren were told to follow their trades. Its teaching is summed up in five principles:

Reverence for God in secret and in public.

Following the *sunna* in word and deed.

Contempt for men in good and bad fortune.

Submission to the will of God in all things, great and small.

Taking refuge in God in joy and sorrow.

The order encourages the use of the good things of this life, even approving service under the government. In its discipline the instructions of the head are adapted to the needs of the novice or brother. Most of its adherents are in Tunis and Algeria.

The 'Isāwī Order. It was founded about 1500. The mother convent is at Meknes in Morocco where the head and his deputy live. A council of forty live like hermits in the convent, leaving it only once a year on the birthday of the prophet. The Shādhilī rule is followed. A ritual dance round a fire often ends with a meal of raw flesh from a ram or goat which has not been skinned. The ritual seems to deaden the sensations of the brethren and they are called in when epidemics occur because it is believed that they can drive out jinn. The order encouraged men to take part in the wars against the Portuguese and Spaniards and also against the later Merinids but since then no political activity is recorded. The order is found in Morocco, Algeria and Tunis.

The Tijānī Order. It was founded in 1782; the members are called friends and must not belong to any other order. The main doctrine is obedience to the government so they have always supported the French.

"It is the aim of the order to live in the quiet of a religious life."

The litany is a hundred repetitions of certain formulas at fixed times in the day. It is spread through French North and West Africa.

The Encyclopaedia of Islam gives a list of one hundred and seventy-five major orders with many branch orders. Here follow a few of the more important with the dates of the founders' deaths and the area of activity.

Aḥmadī. †1276. Egypt.

Burhānī. †1277. Egypt.

Jazūlī. A Moroccan reform of the Shādhilī.

Darkāwa. †1823. Algeria and Morocco. Branch of the Jazūlī.

Jalwatī. †1580. Turkey.

Suhrawardī. †1167 and †1234. India. (Two founders.)

Khalwatī. †1397. Turkey. Branch of the Suhrawardī.
Kubrāwī. †1221. Khorasan.
Madārī. †1438. A peripatetic Indian order.
Mawlawī (Mevlevī) †1273. Asia Minor.
Rifā'ī. †1175. South Iraq.
Ni'matullāhī. †1430. The only Persian Order.

The Shī'a disapproves of the orders because they introduced novelties into Islam and their teaching removed the imams from their place in the centre of the religious life.

The mystic felt himself superior to the scholars who drew their learning from books; they followed earthly teachers, he learnt direct from God. No reliance can be put in the faith of one who believes because of proofs for it is built on speculation and can be demolished by criticism. Quite different is the intuitive faith of the heart which cannot be refuted. Some mystics went so far as to mock at reason and the knowledge based on it. Similarly, obedience to God, enthusiastic because based on love, was better than the calculated casuistry of the lawyers.

The early ascetics were constant in the observance of prayer and the other religious duties. Later some teachers explained these duties allegorically. Among the mystics there was a tendency to regard them as a preliminary to the religious life, to assume that communion with God was a higher form of worship. From this position it was only a step to believe that these external duties were not binding on the adept, that they were only a schoolmaster to lead men to the life of the spirit. The consciousness of union with God raised the mystic above the limits of Islam; he made a show of revering its laws but all rituals and confessions are but an outer husk compared to the love of God.

> When the image of our beloved is in the temple of an idol, it is vain to march round the Ka'ba; when the Ka'ba has lost its fragrance, it is a synagogue; and when in the synagogue we perceive the fragrance of our union with Him, it is our Ka'ba.

Some went further and said that no law was binding on the

adept. The division of the orders into two classes 'with the law' and 'without the law' is well established. The Malāmatīs, like the Cynics, thought it their duty to shock folks by acts that no respectable man would dream of doing, so to earn for themselves the condemnation of others and to be regarded as transgressors of the law even when they kept it carefully. They desired the scorn of others to show their indifference to what men might think.

A famous teacher deserves a less summary treatment. Muḥyī-l-dīn Ibn al-'Arabi was the most systematic thinker among the mystics—so far as they are systematic. He was a thorough monist; the only reality is God; the universe is His expression of Himself. Reality is one with two aspects; being is *ḥaqq* when regarded as the essence of all things; it is creation when regarded as the objects and phenomena which manifest the essence. (Actually there is no such act as creation; but the word is convenient.) The universe does not proceed from God by emanations but by manifestations; He makes Himself known to Himself in everything. Owing to our finite minds and our inability to grasp the whole as a whole, we regard it as a plurality, ascribing to each unit a character which distinguishes it from everything else; only the mystic in a supra-mental state of intuition can transcend the multiplicity of forms and perceive the reality underlying them. God hears and sees in every being which sees and hears, and this is His immanence; His essence is not limited to any one being or group of beings but is manifested in all beings; He is above all limitation and individualization; this is His transcendence. The mystic does not become one with God; he becomes conscious of his oneness with Him.

The light of Muḥammad was the first manifestation of God. It is more than a revelation which, incarnated in the prophets, led men back and upwards to God; it is a cosmic principle which unites all phenomena into the manifestation of the real.

It is obvious that in this system all religions are on one level; the worshipper of fire worships one aspect of the real which is the only good. The gnostic alone can look behind the plurality of appearances. The only evil is not-being. Things, which seem to be unpleasant and bad, seem to be so because ignorant man cannot fit them into their place in the universe. Man is not a moral agent—though Ibn al-'Arabi tries to avoid this conclusion—he just works out the laws which govern his being. It is the will of God that we should have ideas of perfection and imperfection, harmony and discord, good and evil, so that we may know the full nature of God and of ourselves. Without such ideas no society could exist or progress.

Another form of mystic speculation results in the doctrine of the Perfect Man. The basic ideas are the same; the unique essence manifesting itself in the plurality of phenomena and the multiplicity striving to return to unity. Pure being has neither name nor attribute, only when it descends from its absoluteness and enters the realm of manifestation do names and attributes appear. This world is no illusion; it is real because it is the self-revelation of the absolute. Being is identical with thought. The created world is the outward of that whose inward is God. Man is the cosmic thought assuming flesh and connecting absolute being with the world of nature. Every appearance shows some aspect of reality; man is the microcosm in which all attributes are united and in him the absolute becomes conscious of itself in all its aspects. The perfect man has fully realized his essential oneness with God in whose likeness he is made; his religious function as mediator between God and man corresponds to his metaphysical function as the unifying principle by which the opposites, reality and appearance, are harmonized. The return from plurality to unity takes place in the unifying experience of his soul. This is the function of the light of Muḥammad.

Much the same was said by others in simpler language.

> When my servant's first thought is of Me, I make his happiness and joy in the thought of Me. Then He loves Me and I love him, take away the veil that is between us, and become his chief concern, though others pay no heed. His word is that of the prophets; he is the true hero; had I wished to punish men, at the thought of him I would avert punishment from them.

God has servants who would put out the fires of hell if they were to spit on them.

These ideas were systematized in another form. At the head of the community stand prophets and below them are saints who are the elect of the mystics. The saints form an invisible hierarchy on which the order of the world depends. The head is the *Quṭb* (pole, axis) and under him are three overseers, four supports, seven pious ones, forty deputies, and three hundred righteous. These form a parliament to the meetings of which they travel with the speed of light, crossing mountains and seas as easily as ordinary men cross a road. These all know each other though they may be unknown to men. If anything goes wrong in the world, one of the greater saints is there to report to the Pole that the defect may be set right. When a Pole dies he is succeeded by one of the overseers. To the same set of ideas belongs the belief in the mysterious Khaḍir who is always wandering over the earth, helping the afflicted.

In the history of mysticism Ghazālī is important and a sketch of his life will be useful. He was a successful teacher of law in Baghdad but gave up his position there because of a crisis in his religious life. He lost his faith, mental trouble was accompanied by physical, and he could no longer teach. In his distress he began again at the beginning and studied religion from all points of view. He started with those aspects of it which could be studied in books, the Koran, tradition, theology and philosophy but none of these helped him. Then he turned to the mystics who were more difficult because their doctrine included a way of life in addition to book learning. In their company he recovered his faith and found peace. He found that the foundation of religion is communion with God. Philosophy was a useful discipline but it could prove nothing, law and theology lost themselves in useless hair-splitting over unimportant details, religious books gave raw material for life but no system, mysticism degenerated into fantasies or pantheism. Ghazālī became the new champion of Islam, demanding the strict observance of its forms and finding in them a means of approach to God. He cast off the extravagances of the mystics and though he heard words which cannot be uttered, he made no attempt to repeat them. He complains that teachers of religion "who construct their God, acknowledging that He is one yet embracing all" do not experience Him. They divide the world into physics and metaphysics and resolve the clash between the one and the many but the sixth sense is not awakened in them. Only through it can they escape the contradiction which a demonstrated concept of God brings with it. They put God outside the world whither no bridge can bring men to Him. It takes them all their time to maintain the unique being and working of God in their science and ethics. When they see that this empiricism is wrong, universal monotheism can become an immediate experience. This experience is not a 'state', to use the language of the mystics.

Ghazālī discovered that the motive of religion is love to God and he won over Islam to his view. Man's perfection and happiness consist in trying to practise the qualities of God and in adorning himself with the real nature of His attributes. Put in other words; the consciousness of the unity and universality of God, when it has penetrated man's feelings and mastered his spirit, makes him act according to the will of the one God.

There was a belief that every hundred years a restorer of religion was sent into the world. Ghazālī was acclaimed as the restorer of his age, the great renewer, the 'Proof of Islam'; henceforward mysticism, rooted on the pillars of Islam, was part of religion.

While Ghazālī wrote books for philosophers, he made a place for intellectual babes who needed milk. Man has to believe in one God who is unique, wise and able to carry out his wishes. Belief is a firm conviction that does not permit of hesitation or doubt. It may be reached in several ways.

1. By exhaustive proof based on sound premises with all steps of the argument carefully tested so that ambiguity and uncertainty are excluded. Only one or two in a generation, if so many, reach this stage. If salvation depended on it, few would be saved.

2. By dialectical and probable arguments based on propositions accepted by the wise which human nature refuses to

doubt. Some acquire a firm conviction by this means.

3. By forensic arguments such as are used in debates and discussions. These will bring conviction to most men so long as they are not hide-bound by prejudice. Most of the arguments in the Koran are of this sort. Anyone who has kept the natural religious spirit and does not argue for argument's sake will be convinced by, "If there were more gods than One, the world had come to ruin".

4. By listening to one who is known to speak the truth.

5. By hearing what the conscience at once accepts. This makes the man-in-the-street believe firmly though a thoughtful man would see that it does not fulfil the conditions for producing knowledge.

6. By hearing what agrees with his character so that he is convinced by it though neither the character of the teller nor external circumstances testify to its truth.

Though such a conviction is not the direct knowledge of the mystic yet it is sufficient, for it leaves on the soul an impression which is in accord with reality so that, when death removes the veil of the flesh, it does not burn with the fire of shame nor in the fire of hell. Elsewhere Ghazālī could say that the ruler ought to suppress some heresies with the sword.

It is instructive to put side by side the ordinary conception of mystic illumination and Ghazāli's version of it. The first runs thus. Once started on the way, the fatigues of which are rewarded by attaining to truth and the goal of which is knowledge though the wayfarer has not wholly acquired it. For he is only now prepared to strive after certainty (*'ilm al-yaqīn*). By concentrating the inward intuition on the one reality he can rise to immediate consciousness of actual certainty (*'ayn al-yaqīn*). At this stage he is independent of human knowledge and instruction; divine knowledge without mediation shines into his soul and he looks on reality. Above this stage is the truth of certainty (*ḥaqq al-yaqīn*) which cannot be attained by mystic discipline.

Ghazālī says: Gnostics, after the ascent to the heaven of reality, are agreed that they saw in existence only the real. To some this state was discursive knowledge; to others it was ecstasy. Plurality was banished from them totally and they were absorbed in pure uniqueness; intelligence came to an end and they were as those bewildered. They could think of nothing but God, not of themselves. Only God remained with them and they were drunk with a drunkenness beyond the sway of their reason. One said, 'I am creative truth', another, 'Praise be to me, how exalted I am', and another, 'In this coat is only God'. The words of lovers when drunk are confused not straightforward but, when the intoxication passes and they come back to the sway of reason, which is God's measuring-stick in the earth, they know that this was not the real unification but only a semblance of it, as the lover said, 'I am he whom I love and he whom I love is I; we are two spirits, we dwell in one body'. He sees wine in a glass and thinks that the wine is the colour of the glass but, when this is familiar to him and he is firmly established in it, he drains it and says, 'The glass is thin, the wine delicious, they are alike and confusion results; it is as if wine were there and no cup, as if a cup but no wine'. He makes a distinction between saying 'the wine is a cup' and 'as if it were the cup'. When this state is overpowering, it is called oblivion (*fanā*) in the mystic, nay, it is the oblivion of oblivion for he is dead to himself and dead to his deadness. In this state he is not conscious of himself nor of not being conscious of himself. Were he conscious of this unconsciousness, he would be conscious of himself. When a man is absorbed in this state, it is called metaphorically, union, and in the language of reality, unity. These realities are secrets into which it is not permitted to delve. Of these he can say, "To divulge the secrets of Lordship is unbelief".

A creed composed in the nineteenth century shows the spread of the mystic spirit; it states that the double confession contains all that a man needs to know of belief in God and His messengers. Muḥammad establishes the validity of his forerunners and the declaration of the unity of God includes all that is meant by faith. Every reasonable man will keep this declaration always in mind, having ever in his thought the teaching involved, till the words and their meaning permeate his flesh and blood so that he thereby sees secrets and wonders that cannot be counted, if God wills.

Illumination. Closely connected with mysticism is the

doctrine of illumination; it is neo-Platonism expressed in terms borrowed from the dualism of light and darkness. The names *ishrāqī* and *mashriqī* both mean the same thing and are a pun, denoting the knowledge that comes from the east and by illumination. The discoverers of it were Hermes, Agathodaimon, the Greek philosophers up to and including Plato and the seers of Persia, who all taught the same doctrine. This is based on revelation and intuition as opposed to Aristotle, the Peripatetics and the theologians whose knowledge is based on argument and proof. There is a greater east, the world of intelligences or pure lights, and a lesser east, the world of souls. The intelligences rise in the eastern horizon of God and the souls in that of the intelligences. To this succession corresponds a succession of descents to the west; and in the return of the soul to its origin lies the appearance of the soul apart from its body, its dawn, and its manifestation, after a purifying discipline, when the world of souls is revealed to it. Later the world of intelligences is revealed to it as it rises from the world of souls which has now become its west. Finally it meets at 'the gate of gates' the first intelligence, the giver from which souls emanate, Gabriel.

Illuminative knowledge is immediate; mediate knowledge, acquired through the medium of an intelligible form, is knowledge of universals only. True knowledge is intuitive, unitary knowledge of the essence in its individuality. In this every veil is taken away and the soul knows the essence because it is present in it. This is only possible when the soul has stripped itself of all material things. The Light of Lights is at once the source of all being and all knowledge, both of which irradiate from it. "Low light, if there is no veil between it and the high, sees the high which lights it. The highest light is lighted by the rays of the Light of Lights."

Victorious lights move the spheres, taking the place of the pure intelligences of other systems. Darkness is only the absence of light; it is caused by barriers (*barzakh*) which shut off the light. The encompassing barrier is the outermost sphere; it is everywhere identical with itself so every point on it is the highest and the centre is the lowest. The living barrier is the heavenly bodies and the dead barrier material bodies.

Illumination is superior to philosophy as mysticism is superior to Islam. The supreme bliss is the knowledge of God in His attributes and His acts and of the beginning and end of being. There are two paths to this goal; the first by reasoning and argument and the second by training and discipline. Those who follow the first path are the Peripatetic philosophers; those who follow the first path and a prophet are the theologians; those who follow the second and Islam are the mystics; and the illuminated follow only the second path. In the first path are degrees, the material reason, reason in act, reason as a habit, and the reason from above which is not to be found in this world. The degrees of the second path are the discipline of the body by following religious laws, the pruning of bad habits from the soul, the polishing of the soul by pure and holy forms and, lastly, concentration on the beauty of God to the exclusion of all else. The third stage of this path, the polishing of the soul, is parallel to the fourth stage of the first path, the reason from above, because both see the images of things known, but differs from it because reason is not free from doubt. Also the soul is like a mirror; with reason only part of it is polished and only part of the universe is reflected in it; but when it is wholly polished, it reflects everything.

This doctrine may be summed up as a spiritualist philosophy with a theory of mystical knowledge; God and the spiritual world are conceived as light and the acquisition of knowledge is illumination from above through the medium of the spirits of the spheres.

CHAPTER VIII

STATE

NOWHERE is the clash between fact and theory more evident than in politics. Muḥammad died leaving no instructions about a successor. A schism between Mecca and Medina was narrowly avoided and Abū Bakr chosen caliph, deputy for Muḥammad. He in turn nominated as his successor ʿUmar who appointed a committee to select the next caliph. ʿAlī tried to get himself accepted by the people of Medina. The authority familiar to the Arabs was that of the tribal chief, a man of great influence but little direct power, who ruled by persuasion and force of personality. Such were the 'orthodox caliphs'. Modern Muslims are fond of calling their rule a republic but this is inexact; the caliphs were ready to listen to any counsellor but did not hesitate to go their own way. The Umayyads were accused of changing the caliphate into a kingdom, and with some justice for they tried to make power hereditary; but the earlier rulers behaved like great Arab chiefs. Even they had to get their chosen heirs acknowledged by the community. The Abbasids did not greatly modify their practice.

The law says that God is the head of the state which He rules through the law; the earthly head, whom the laws calls imam, is merely an executive to enforce the law, a political and social necessity. Some argued that as the office of imam had been the cause of strife it might be wise to do without one and be content with the law alone. It was assumed that he would be chosen by the leaders of the community and a second assumption was that these leaders were the learned in the law. He had to fulfil eleven conditions, among them these: he must be an adult male Muslim, belong to the tribe of Quraish, be in full possession of all his faculties, not a cripple, and be learned in the Koran and law. The majority say that he must be the most worthy of his time for the post; some waived this condition if the most worthy had refused the office. It is not a condition of his appointment that he should be infallible and without sin; indeed he must not be removed from office when he does wrong. A hidden imam, such as the Shīʿa believe in, is useless because he cannot do his duty. His functions are to preserve religion in its original purity, to see that the law is obeyed and the penalties decreed by God inflicted, to defend the frontiers, equip the army and make the necessary payments from the treasury regularly but without extravagance, to collect the taxes, to keep down violent men, thieves and brigands, to maintain the Friday and festival prayers, to settle disputes, to receive witness about people's rights, to marry minors both boys and girls who have no guardians, to divide booty, to appoint trustworthy men to office, and to take personal share in the business of the state, giving it full attention.

Some held that the need for a head of the state was made known by revelation, others that it was known by reason only. The Shīʿa say that caliph is a more general term than imam and so call the first three rulers caliphs but not imams; others tended to make imam the more general term. In matters political the *sunnīs* practically equate them.

Though the caliphs lost their temporal power, somewhat of their old prestige clung to them. Generals, who had carved out for themselves kingdoms, sought legitimation for what they had done by getting a diploma of investiture from the caliph, among such were Maḥmūd of Ghazni, Saladin and some rulers of Delhi. The caliph was more and more isolated, a miniature shows him riding with his officers, his face veiled.

The Fatimid caliph sometimes preached the Friday sermon but always from behind a screen. The title 'shadow of God on earth' became common. A modern Muslim explains this as an influence of western thought and an attempt to assimilate the caliph to the pope.

To the lawyers the appointment of a caliph is a contract between two parties, the ruler and the subjects; if the ruler goes mad, becomes blind, adopts another religion, or is taken prisoner by men of another faith, the contract is broken and a new caliph must be elected.

Administration of Justice

It is not easy to give a plain account as the spheres of the various authorities overlap. There is no distinction of civil from criminal jurisdiction so all cases may come before the judge. He must be an upright man and learned in the law; usually he followed one of the four schools though some gave decisions according to two or even more schools. Every big town had its judge. In early times those in the provinces were appointed by the governor, only occasionally by the caliph. He held his court in his own house or in the mosque; some held that he ought not to sit in the mosque as non-Muslims could not approach him there. Non-Muslims appeared before him in cases against Muslims or of their own choice; in the latter case they elected to be judged by Muslim law. The plaintiff had to produce evidence while the defendant was allowed to clear himself by oath. The judge was assisted by witnesses who originally testified to the character of the parties and not to the facts. They were more or less officials and came to perform some of the minor duties of the judge; we read of a witness being rejected because he played chess. As a rule the judge cannot act till one or both parties to a case call him in; if it is a matter of religion, he can act on his own initiative. The law being what it is, it is easy to see that the boundary line between the two classes is vague; thus, obstructions to a highway come under the head of religious matters.

In a big town there may be two or more judges representing different schools; there was an army judge and one accompanied the pilgrim caravan. The judge, or senior judge, in the capital was chief justice with some kind of supervision over the other judges. Hārūn Rashīd was the first to appoint a supreme judge in Damascus; four, one for each school, were set up in Cairo towards the end of the Crusades and in Damascus in 1266. Further the judge is guardian of orphans, idiots, and those who have been restrained by law from control of their own affairs, if they have no natural guardian. This includes arranging suitable marriages for his wards. He is also supervisor of religious and charitable foundations (*waqf*) and has to see that they serve the objects for which they were created; he has to watch over wills to see that they do not infringe the law and that the provisions in them are carried out.

Subordinate appointments made by a judge lapsed at his death.

Complaints (*maẓālim*). The extraordinary jurisdiction of the sovereign is described in the chapter on law.

The muftī. In the early centuries scholarship was not organized; usually scholars lived in cities but this was not the invariable rule. A man got a reputation for learning and students went to him wherever he might be. Learning came to mean knowledge of Islam, more particularly, of the law. A man troubled by a case of conscience took his problem to a scholar and accepted his answer as the solution of his difficulty. Such a scholar was a *muftī* and his answer was a *fatwā*. Two parties could go to a judge whose decision was binding or they could go by agreement to a *muftī* and abide by his ruling. By the year 1000 some *muftīs* had become officials and were present when the monarch or his deputy 'sat for complaints'. About 1400 there were two in Damascus, a Shāfi'ī and a Ḥanafī. The *muftī* was below the judge in rank yet the judge would state a case to the *muftī* and accept his decision.

The chief *muftī* of Constantinople became a most important person; European travellers compare him to a cardinal or even to the pope. His importance seems to have grown and did not come from a delegation of power by the sultan. He was given the title Shaikh of Islam and it was his duty to see that laws proposed by the sultan did not contradict the law of Islam. An upright shaikh of Islam could and did oppose the sultan. More than once when a sultan wished to exterminate or banish all Christians from the empire, the shaikh forbade him because they were under the protection of the sacred law which guaranteed their lives and the free exercise of their religion so long as they paid the necessary taxes and did nothing to betray the state. About 1620 the sultan deprived the holder of the office of all his powers because he would not sanction the murder of the sultan's brother, but they were restored in the next reign. In 1632 the sultan had the shaikh of Islam murdered but this did not affect the importance of the office. In 1909 when it was proposed to depose the sultan, the shaikh was asked for a *fatwā* declaring that the deposition was lawful. The Turks also appointed a chief muftī in Egypt. In Persia the shaikhs of Islam were officials who presided over the religious courts in the big towns.

The Muḥtasib. He was inspector of markets and censor of morals. It was his duty to see that public worship was duly maintained, public order was not disturbed, that traders used correct weights and measures, and sold pure and unadulterated goods. He could restrain teachers whose doctrines were subversive of Islam and prevent licentious books being read in schools. Speaking generally, he was subordinate to the judge but he could often act on his own initiative whereas the judge could only act when a case was brought to him; but if there was a conflict of evidence, the *muḥtasib* had to refer the case to the judge.

If a man drank wine in public, he was asking for trouble; if he got drunk in private, however much the *muḥtasib* might suspect, he could not violate the privacy of the man's house and take him in the act. The law was often reasonable.

Several manuals for holders of this office exist, they throw much light on the commercial life of the period and it is clear that a conscientious *muḥtasib* had to know much about the shady side of life if he were to do his duty.

Chief of the Police

'Uthmān, the third caliph, was killed because there was no garrison in Medina to protect him. The Umayyad caliphs repaired this error and protected themselves with a bodyguard; their provincial governors did likewise. These troops. were the *shurṭa* and the commander was the *ṣāḥib al-shurṭa* These soldiers carried out some of the duties of police. The commander in the capital was a most important person if the succession to the throne was disputed; in the absence of the caliph he was practically his deputy. He became an established part of the legal machine though canon law never recognized his existence. The functions and difficulties of this office are set out in the following history. Ḥajjāj appointed a man to this office but he refused to accept it till the caliph had promised to support him against the governor's family and retainers. The

H

story goes on: "He did not imprison except for debt (or religion, the unvocalized text is ambiguous); if a man broke into a house, his belly was pierced by a spike which came out at his back; a robber of graves had a grave dug for him and he was buried in it; one who had fought with a sword or knife had his hand cut off; he who set fire to a house was burned; a doubtful character who could not be proved a thief got three hundred lashes." This list shows the difference between the duties of the chief of police and those of the *muḥtasib* better than any definition.

Story-teller Preacher

At first many Muslims knew little of their religion so pious men took upon themselves to instruct the ignorant, often with official sanction. The first Umayyad caliph appointed a man to lecture after the morning and evening prayers; he glorified God, pronounced a blessing on the prophet, prayed for the caliph, his court and army, and the people of Syria and cursed his enemies and all unbelievers. Such men were called story-tellers (*qāṣṣ*) though hedge-preachers would describe them better. They accompanied an army which gathered to avenge Ḥusain, teaching and exhorting the troops. In Egypt during the seventh and eighth centuries the judge was often also the preacher. One had a double audience; he read a verse of the Koran, explained it in Arabic to the Arabs who sat on one side and then in Persian to the Persians who sat on the other side. His Arabic and Persian were equally good. Gradually the preachers split into two classes, the scholars who were more or less official and the popular who tickled the ears of their audience. These brought the profession into discredit; they are grouped with those who exhibited trained monkeys and bears. One, for instance, told his hearers that a believer would have in paradise a house, three thousand miles long, broad and high, with doors thirty miles high and wide. "Not a house for January", said a profane listener. Muslims say that these men are responsible for the extravagances of popular belief; e.g. that when Muḥammad ascended to heaven God told him not to take off his shoes because heaven was honoured by the touch of them.

There are two names for mosque; *masjid* suggests worship and *jāmi'* a meeting-house; *masjid jāmi'* is one where the midday prayer on Friday is celebrated. In the early days the mosque served for all public meetings as well as worship. The caliph or governor issued declarations of policy there; it seems that meetings for secular purposes were summoned by the call to prayer. Opposition to the government came into the open there as riot or rebellion. Travellers lodged there. Teachers, not of religion only, held their classes there; a well-known man had his special place where he sat against a pillar with a ring of students round him. The accredited witnesses, who served as notaries, sometimes had their seats in the mosque and the judge might hold his court there. Since then customs have not changed much. The sermon on Friday has become a formality, for the most part; an Indian schoolboy was allowed to recite the sermon because he had learnt a little Arabic. A big mosque has several officials, the muezzin (*mu'adhdhin*) who gives the call to prayer, the preacher (*khaṭīb*), and the leader of worship (*imām*) who receive salaries. In the Middle Ages these were often scholars of repute. In a small mosque almost anyone may perform these duties. A mosque is often endowed with *waqf* property; it is common to find one surrounded with shops that belong to it, the rents providing for the upkeep.

The word *waqf* was used in connection with the mosque. Two definitions may be given; the appropriation of a particular article in such a manner as subjects it to the rules of divine property whence the appropriator's right in it is extinguished and it becomes the property of God by the advantage of it resulting to His creatures; and, it is the immobilization of the usufruct of a thing for a term equal to the duration of that thing. It is the only form of perpetuity known to Islam and is irrevocable. 'Charitable trust' is a reasonably satisfactory translation. Perishable goods and money (prohibition of interest) cannot be made a trust. A trust cannot be used for a purpose unpleasing to God; e.g. a man cannot so treat his property to escape payment of his debts and a Christian cannot make a trust for a mosque or a church, for the former is contrary to his own religion and the second contrary to Islam.

Practically trusts fall into two classes, public and private.

The public are for true charitable purposes, the maintenance of worship, including the upkeep of the fabric of mosques and payment of ministers of religion, and charities including works of public utility such as hospitals, schools, water supply and anything of a like nature. According to Ḥanafī law, a private mosque built by a rich man for his own worship cannot be the object of a trust because it is not a public utility.

Private trusts are those intended to preserve family property from the rapacity of authority or to evade the law of inheritance as laid down in the Koran which would split up the estate. The beneficiaries are the founder's descendants and collaterals. According to Ḥanafī law, the maintenance of the founder for his life and the payment of his debts may be the first charges on the trust. A trust has to have a manager; the founder may appoint himself or another to this post. Ḥanafī law says that he may retain the usufruct for his life but he cannot encumber even the use and enjoyment beyond the term of his own life.

Trusts dealt mostly with real property, at first with houses only but later agricultural land was allowed. As this land was let on short lease, usually for one year, the trusts were a danger to the community especially when they became extensive. In the later Middle Ages a Government department controlled the public trusts while the private were under the supervision of the chief judge who could remove a manager if he failed in his duty. Books given to a mosque or library were often made a trust. Trusts existed in many lands for the benefit of the holy cities, Mecca and Medina.

The lawyers tried to prove that Muḥammad and the Companions created trusts. In fact, the institution developed during the first two centuries and was probably suggested by Byzantine customs, especially the estates owned by churches.

Revenue. In addition to the legal alms Muslim landowners paid a tax on crops called tithe; it was ten per cent, but if the crop was irrigated from wells, it was five per cent of the crop. Christian Arabs paid double this amount while *dhimmīs* paid a land tax which might be two-fifths or half the crop. This tithe was sometimes called *ṣadaqa* like the legal alms. It was agreed that Arabia was tithe land. Outside Arabia opinions and customs varied. Usually land granted to Muslims, or waste land brought under cultivation by them was tithe land and the same privilege was granted to land bought by them; though on this point opinions varied. The state could release land from the land tax and let it pay tithe only. Converts to Islam expected to be treated like other Muslims but the state did not agree; the resulting struggles belong to history. Some held that only cereals, dates, and orchards paid one or other of these taxes; others affirmed that a handful of greenstuff was taxable. Today in some places in South Arabia the corn is piled in a heap and one-tenth is set on one side; the servants of the saint take half and his descendants take the other half. Elsewhere so many furrows are set apart for the saint. *Dhimmīs* paid also a poll tax, according to their wealth, one, two, or four dinars yearly or the equivalent in dirhams. The State took one-fifth from mines, treasure trove, and what was cast up by the sea, pearls or ambergris. There was also a tax on trade; Muslims paid two and a half per cent, *dhimmīs* five per cent, and foreigners ten per cent of the value of the goods. Quantities below ten dinars in value were free.

The Citizens

The interest of this section is mostly historical. Only Muslims could be full citizens. Jews and Christians might live in the state if they paid poll tax and behaved loyally; this privilege was soon extended to the fire worshippers of Persia and later, under stress of circumstances, to the Hindus. They were called "those under the protection of God and His Apostle", and for short, "the people of the protection" (*ahl ul-dhimma*), or by the adjective *dhimmī*. The official salutation to them was, "Greeting to those who follow the guidance". In the early days Christian Arabs did not pay the poll tax but paid double the taxes paid by Muslims; this class soon disappeared. Under the law that there was only one religion in Arabia, the *dhimmīs* were banished from the peninsula but were allowed to visit it for purposes of trade. At first the Arab conquerors were marked off from the provincials by appearance and dress. As progress in civilization and intermarriage blurred the difference, it was laid down that *dhimmīs* should wear a distinctive dress, a girdle, a coloured patch on the outer garment and a turban, usually blue for the

Christian, yellow for the Jew. As late as 1800 they were not allowed on the pavements in Damascus.

Normally they did not serve in the army. In theory they might keep their places of worship in repair but might not build new ones, especially in towns that were peculiarly Arab like Basra and Kufa. Much however depended on the temper of the Government. They might not parade their religion before Muslims, blasphemy against Muḥammad was punished with death, even criticism of him met with severe chastisement. They were forbidden to build houses higher than those of Muslims because so much of the daily life, night life would be more correct, is spent on the roof. The law says that no one, who is not a Muslim, may exercise authority over Muslims but necessity made it a dead letter. *Dhimmīs* were always to be found in Government offices and in the service of private persons, acting as clerks and secretaries. It is said that the Coptic clerks in the Egyptian ministries safeguarded themselves by making the Government accounts so complicated that no one else could understand them. Again and again the ruler decreed that all *dhimmīs* should be dismissed from public and private employ but they always came back. When they forgot their precarious position and became tyrannical, as they often did, the result was a riot with plunder, arson and murder. They might not own Muslim slaves; if the slave of a *dhimmī* turned Muslim, he had to be sold to a Muslim. In the Ottoman Empire the theory was that the *dhimmīs* paid extra taxes because they were exempt from military service.

In the modern Arab states citizenship does not depend on religion. At the beginning of the agitation for Egyptian independence enthusiastic manifestations of brotherhood between the Muslims and the Christian Copts took place. In Iraq the amendment of 1943 to the organic law declared that Iraqis are all equal in respect of rights and duties. No distinction is to be made between them on grounds of race, language or religion. Nothing like this can be said of Arabia.

Education

"Seek knowledge even if it be from China"; Muslim scholarship is too famous to need any introduction. At first the mosque was the place where teaching was given, not only in religious subjects but also in secular such as poetry and literature. About the year 800 a 'house of wisdom' was built in Baghdad with a library, staff to look after it, and arrangements for students. An observatory was connected with it. Two hundred years later a similar institution was erected in Cairo, largely for Shī'a propaganda. Private persons founded similar libraries; early in the tenth century a man established a school and library with dwellings and allowances in money for the students. Salaried teachers are also mentioned. Some lectured on law in their own houses. About the same time schools (*madrasa*) began to be founded, often for a famous teacher. After 1000, such schools became numerous, the best known being the Niẓāmiya in Baghdad which was dedicated in 1067; the founder is said to have established a school in every town in Iraq and Khurasan. To begin with, the Niẓāmiya had only one teacher but others were soon appointed. Law was the main subject; a small school might be Ḥanafī or Shāfi'ī while a big school would have teachers for each of the four schools of law. Other religious subjects were often added to the curriculum. A school of grammar is heard of. The mosque still maintained itself as a place of teaching; a man might lecture in a school on law and in a mosque on the Koran. Some schools even included a hospital. The distinction between mosque and *madrasa* was often slight, especially when the *madrasa* contained the grave of its founder. There was always a place for prayer which, in later times, often had a pulpit for the Friday prayers. The foundation of Sultan Ḥasan in Cairo was both mosque and *madrasa*.

The earlier method of instruction was dictation; the teacher read a passage from a text and then commented on it, the students writing as he spoke. Sometimes there was an assistant (*mustamlī*) to read the text or this task might be given to a student. Great freedom in asking questions was allowed. There might be other assistants (*mu'īd*, literally repeater) who went over the day's work with the less gifted students. Later on the practice of dictation lapsed and the teacher lectured freely. After studying a text with his teacher a student received a licence (*ijāza*) to teach it; when such a licence went back by a series of teachers to the author of the book it was highly prized. There was also a general licence to teach all the works of the master. The licence system was abused; children in arms were taken to hear a famous teacher. The boundary between teacher and student was not sharply drawn; a man might be teacher in one subject and student in another. The teachers were organized in some way; about 800 a man in Egypt held the chieftainship of the teachers which presumes some organization though the details are not known.

A strong feeling existed that a teacher, especially of religion, ought not to take pay for his services. A teacher fell into a well and when men came to pull him out, he insisted that none who had heard his teaching of the Koran or tradition should help lest he should lose his reward from God for teaching. Most saw no harm in paying a teacher though some said that he ought not to fix his fee but take what was offered. Later, however, it was usual for teachers to be paid from the endowments of the institution. Still later the emoluments of both teachers and students were reckoned in loaves of bread. Some earned their living by trade or profession, it is enough to mention a weaver, a bookbinder and an engraver of gems.

The subjects studied were classified in two ways. First as those connected with religion and those not so connected.

1. Connected with religion, *naqlī* (founded on revelation); they are those concerned with the Koran, the recitation of the sacred book (*tajwīd*), the readings, and interpretation, then tradition with the relevant facts about the reporters (*'ilm al-rijāl*) and the abrogating and abrogated verses, law and the principles of law, dogmatic theology and religious observances. As Arabic is the language of the Koran, all studies that aided the understanding of the book came under this head; they are grammar, rhetoric, lexicography, literature and prosody. Further, mathematics and astronomy are needed to calculate the direction of Mecca (*qibla*) and for the division of inheritances.

2. Those not connected with religion; they are called ancient studies, natural, philosophical, foreign or *'aqlī* (founded on reason). They are logic, theory of numbers, geometry,

astronomy, music—the study of tones and the determination of them by number, natural sciences, i.e. the study of bodies in rest and motion, bodies heavenly, human, vegetable, animal and mineral, including medicine and agriculture, and metaphysics.

Philosophy soon disappeared from the mosques; in Spain philosophy and the science of the stars were taught only in secret because adepts in these subjects were suspected of being free thinkers (*zindīq*).

The subjects were also divided into main and auxiliary.

1. The main subjects are theology, ethics, law, principles of law, the Koran and tradition.

2. The auxiliary are grammar, rhetoric, prosody, logic, methodology, mathematics and the terminology of tradition. It seems that even medicine was taught in the mosque; the procedure would have been that of any other subject for religious respect for the human body prevented experiment and the development of anatomy. Even today when a post-mortem has been performed, all parts of the body must be buried together in readiness for the resurrection.

Respect for the teacher was great; the boy's father was responsible for his body coming into being but the teacher was responsible for his mind. It was better to go wrong after a teacher than to go right without one. This was inculcated by the law which said that game caught by a trained dog was lawful food but that caught by one untrained was not lawful.

Many held that education was not for women, that an educated woman was a danger to her husband. That this view was not universal is shown by the biographical dictionaries of the thirteenth to the fifteenth centuries where hundreds of women scholars are named, particularly as students and teachers of tradition.

Oddly enough teachers of children were despised; they spent their days with children and their nights with women. A teacher, the son of a teacher, was asked, "Why are you a fool?" He replied, "If I were not a fool, I should be illegitimate". A judge laid down this rule:

When a teacher of children says, 'The Jews are much

> better than the Muslims for they fulfil their obligations to the teachers of their children', anyone who so speaks is to be regarded as an unbeliever.

The rule that a teacher must be married and must not keep school in his own house throws a fierce light on the morals of the time.

CHAPTER IX

SOCIAL LIFE AND POPULAR IDEAS

THE brotherhood of Islam is a real thing, the religion does unite its adherents. Theology says that God is so great that all men are equal before Him, being His slaves; this equality is most apparent in the mosque though it is not absolute even there. Social divisions exist. In South Arabia the sayyids, tribesmen, merchants and *akhdām*, who are a servile class mostly of mixed African descent, are separate classes which do not mix. In India Muslims are divided into high and low classes, castes might be a better name. The high are four, after the Hindu model; sayyids are descendants of the prophet, shaikhs are of Arab descent, Mughal includes those connected with the rulers of Delhi and Turks, and Pathans who come from the North-west Frontier or Afghanistan. The claims expressed by these names are largely imaginary. The low classes are converts from low Hindu castes or outcasts. In some places these are not admitted into the mosques nor into the cemeteries after death.

In the first century of Islam there are traces of a colour bar; for the time of Hārūn Rashīd an historian argues that no self-respecting Arab woman, let alone the caliph's sister, would have dreamed of marrying a Persian and a later caliph was ready to marry a woman from the family of the Seljuk sultans but would not give his daughter to the sultan. Nowadays the northern bedouin do not marry slaves but the chiefs of Asir cannot be distinguished from negroes.

Society where the women are unveiled does not differ appreciably from similar society in Europe. Not so long ago convention insisted that a woman must have her hair covered if only with a net. For earlier times this section can deal only with the society of men. They were careful not to expose their bodies. A man left a charge in his will that his corpse was to be washed through a cloth. When Nimrod tried to burn Abraham, he was stripped and thrown into the fire but Gabriel brought him a shirt of the silk of paradise. When Ibn Ḥanbal was flogged, his clothes began to slip down so a golden hand appeared and held them in place. But talk is often unrestrained, even in the presence of boys, for the processes of nature are natural and can be discussed. Contradictions appear; an Indian divine objected to students reading two lines of Arabic verse describing a woman's body yet he saw no harm in small boys knowing all about the legal impurity of women for ignorance of this might invalidate his prayers.

A passage in the Koran is almost a code of morals:

> Thy Lord has decreed that ye shall not serve ought but Him; and to parents kindness. . . . And give the kinsman his due, and the poor and the wayfarer. But do not lavish wastefully. Do not keep thy hand fettered to thy neck, nor yet stretch it to full width. . . . And slay not your children in fear of poverty. We will provide for them. Beware; to slay them is a great sin. And approach not to fornication; it has always been vileness and evil as a practice. And slay not the soul that God has made inviolable, save for just cause. As for him that is slain unjustly, we have given his representative authority. But let him not exceed in slaying; he shall be aided. And approach not the possessions of the orphan, except for what may be better, until he reach his full strength. And fulfil your compact. Verily your compact shall be required. And give full measure when you measure and weigh with just balance. This is best and most excellent in (its) interpretation. And make no charges of foul deeds where thou hast no knowledge; verily, hearing, sight and mind, all these shall be questioned about it. And walk not on the earth with self-conceit; thou wilt neither split the earth nor touch the mountains in height.

Perhaps the belief is general that a pleasant untruth is better for both parties than an unpalatable truth. It is commonly said that lies may be told in three circumstances, to save one who is hiding from a wicked ruler, to bring about the defeat of unbelievers in war, and to keep the peace between a man and his wife. On the other hand it is written:

> Keep to the truth; for a sharp sword in the hands of a brave man is not more powerful than the truth. And the truth is an honour even if it contain that which you dislike; a lie is humiliation even if it involve something dear to you. Moreover, he that is known to lie is suspect even when telling the truth.

The host says to the guest, "My house is your house," and conveys the impression that it is not a mere form. A Muslim of good breeding is an ornament to the name of gentleman.

Ethics. Morality as taught by the learned is practically Greek; the cardinal virtues are four and the right conduct is the golden mean. Common sense opposes the extremes of trust in God as taught by some mystics; the right thing is to have a year's store of food in the house, more than this is extravagance and less is akin to poverty. The man, who boasted of his perpetual devotions during the pilgrimage, was asked the pertinent question, "Who cooked your food?" The following condemns another aspect of the mystic trust. Guests came to a man who set before them the best he had, dry bread. One of the guests exclaimed, "This would go down well with dried herbs". The host pawned the basin and ewer used for washing the hands before and after meat, bought the herbs and set them before his guests. When they had eaten, one said, "Praise be to God who has satisfied us". This was too much for the host, who cried out, "Would that He had, then I need not have pawned my ewer and basin".

Others saw life as the activity of the three souls. The vegetal was concerned with the upkeep of the body and the continuation of the race; if this was allowed a free hand, the man was sunk in carnal pleasures and lusts. The animal was responsible for the defence of the body against enemies and produced pride and egoism; left to itself, it caused strife between individuals and nations. The rational soul must rule over the other two and then it will create an upright, peaceable man who seeks to uphold the community in the wisdom imparted by God through the prophets. Muslim ethics are social; the Arab idea, which submerged the individual in the tribe, survives in a sublimated form. Man is a microcosm; as reason rules in him by divine wisdom subduing unruly passions, so the monarch rules the state by divine law and every citizen has his part to play in the body politic. If they fail in their duty to the head and to one another, the end is destruction.

Opinions on human nature differed. Some held that a man was born with a definite character and could not change it. Others that education and training could make anyone into a saint. Others again took up a middle position and held that the bias given by birth could be increased or corrected, as might be necessary, by discipline. A tradition says that everyone is born into natural religion and his parents make him a Jew, Christian or Muslim. Some held that virtue was knowledge and an appeal to reason was sufficient to lead anyone into the right path.

The following list of grave sins (it is not the only one) is illuminating for it shows the confused nature of Muslim ethics. Unbelief is the greatest sin of all, murder, unlawful sexual relations—this is illustrated by a tradition, "thou shalt not commit adultery with the wife of a man under thy protection", sodomy, wine bibbing, theft and forcible appropriation of the property of others, slandering honest women (another says that slandering a young girl, a slave woman and one careless of her reputation are venial sins), scandal-mongering, false witness, swearing falsely, failure to do one's duty to one's family or tribe, deserting from the army in the holy war, mismanaging the estate of an orphan, being too early or too late with prayer, telling lies about the prophet, striking a Muslim without due cause, cursing the Companions, concealing testimony, bribery to deflect the course of justice, serving as pimp or pander, delation, refusal to pay the legal alms, despairing of God's mercy, trust in one's cunning and God's pardon of one's sin, violation of *ẓihār*—a formula of divorce which makes subsequent re-marriage equivalent to incest, eating pork or carrion, not fasting in Ramaḍān, cheating, brigandage, sorcery and usury, and persistence in venial sin.

It is noteworthy that there is no mention of suicide. The reason may be that it happened so rarely; in one of the few cases known it is explained that the man was a convert, not a born Muslim.

It is the duty of the Muslim to do his share in maintaining public order; in the words of the Koran he must "command what is right and forbid what is wrong". According to circumstances and his ability he should do this with his sword, his stick, his tongue or his prayers. The word for 'right' in this phrase of the Koran may also mean 'kind deed' and is connected with one of the names for customary as opposed to sacred law; it means primarily 'known' and the word for 'wrong' means 'strange'. The language is a survival from primitive morality where right and wrong are the things done or not done by decent folk.

Respect for the aged and parents has become second nature. A grown-up son would wait on his father and his father's guests at meals, would stand in his presence till commanded to sit, and would not smoke before him. A disobedient son is typical of the incorrigible offender.

Among the virtues praised in literature are the ability to keep a secret and *ḥilm*. This is usually translated 'clemency' but it is more than that; it is self-control and the art of getting one's own way by persuasion instead of using force. The man, who can keep the peace among his wives and household by words alone, has *ḥilm* while one, who has to use the stick or the slipper, is without it. In accord with his usual practice Muḥammad condemned the extravagant generosity which the pagans had praised. The greatest change which he made in moral ideas was his demand for humility before God. The tribes of Central and North Arabia had not paid much attention to God; each thought his own tribe the best and himself the best of his tribe and had no hesitation in saying so. One of their objections to Islam was the attitude in prayer which expressed this humility. To them forgiveness had been weakness and blood revenge a duty; Muḥammad sought to change this. Blood revenge was too deeply rooted in the Arab character to be eradicated entirely, the tribe that was content to take milk when it might have blood—to compound for revenge by blood wit in camels—was despised. It was not necessary to kill the offender, any member of his tribe would do. Muḥammad warned the avenger (*walī*) not to slay indiscriminately, practically to be content with a life for a life but he urged the acceptance of the blood wit. The offender would also expiate his crime of manslaughter by setting a slave free or by a fast of two months. A murderer would be punished by God in hell. Among the bedouin blood revenge still holds; a boy fired the pistol which executed his father's murderer while the boy's uncle steadied his hand. There is some conscience about these matters. A man was killed; one of the dead man's tribe met a fellow tribesman of the slayer before the news spread and killed him. This was felt to be wrong for the second victim knew nothing of what had happened and so had no chance or reason to escape or defend himself.

Decorum is important; a man should be dressed suitably to his rank and the occasion. Eating in public places is reprobated; this is in part due to fear of the evil eye and in part to religious scruple for a man should not be seen eating what others cannot afford to buy. As we have seen a tradition condemns overmuch laughter.

At first the legal alms went to the poor; later it is to be feared that it went into the treasury. In Arabic one word meant both noble and generous. History and literature are full of fantastic tales of open-handed giving and there must be some truth behind them. When colleges were built, they were endowed to provide stipends for the students and often a school for orphan children was attached. Hospitals also provided food as well as drugs and treatment. A common form of good work was to build a fountain or reservoir where the traveller might find water.

Uncleanness. Dogs are unclean, sheep and hunting dogs excepted. A tradition adds those kept by peasants for guarding their fields but a critic remarked that the narrator of the tradition was a farmer.

Certain things are unclean in themselves, pork, carrion, and blood, so must not be used for food. Carrion is defined as any animal which has been killed by another or by accident or has died a natural death. Some even said that the skin of such an animal was unclean and might not be used though others held that tanning purified it. Blood is forbidden as food in the Old Testament but there is no reason to suppose that Muslim practice is borrowed from the Jews. The name for wine *khamr* is a loan word from Aramaic and grape wine was seldom made in Arabia where fermented drinks (*nabīdh*) were made from dates, honey and other substances. It was a matter of debate whether these local drinks were included in the prohibition of wine. In early days *nabīdh* was freely drunk, it was even supplied at the pilgrimage. Later general agreement was reached that all intoxicants were forbidden though many, including caliphs, drank freely. This tale is told to show the evil in wine. A man wanted a certain woman and she agreed to be his if he would commit one of three sins. He chose what he believed to be the least and got drunk; while he was drunk, he committed the other two.

The flesh of all animals which have not been slaughtered in accord with the law is unclean. Details differ in the different schools of law, the essential is that the throat should be cut in such a way that the blood drains from the body. Fish are clean, even those left on the shore by the ebb, because the taking them out of the water is slaughter. Opinions differed whether this was true of all living creatures in the sea and also of dead fish found floating on the surface. Game caught by dogs trained for the purpose was clean even if the animal died before its throat could be cut. The milk of animals which could not be used for food was not clean. The prevalent opinion is that the flesh of the domestic ass may not be eaten. The Arabs eat the big lizards found in their land though Muḥammad himself did not like them. In an emergency anything eatable is lawful. It was debated whether a starving man might eat carrion to satiety or only enough to keep himself alive.

Till recently everybody ate with his fingers so the hands were washed before and after meals. In the desert washing is often omitted and after eating the hands are wiped on the tent wall before the door. A thick coat of grease there is a mark of honour, a proof of the hospitality and generosity of the owner of the tent. The men eat first and then the women and children though it often happens that a man has a favourite son, or daughter, if she is very young, beside him at meal-times. The left hand must not be used in eating; it is employed for unclean purposes. An Englishwoman, guest of a Muslim, inadvertently put her left hand in a dish of pigeons. The host was too well bred to say anything but he looked thunder and upset the dish.

Food might become impure by contact with something unclean. If a man took his religion seriously, all his food had to be clean; there must be no taint in its ancestry, no blot on its scutcheon. To take an extreme example; a man bought selected corn, washed it, sowed it in ground which he had selected, ground it and made bread from it himself. He had clean pottery for his eating and drinking. (The historian adds that he went mad and claimed to be caliph though he recovered later.) Another ate only what was given him by a friend on the lawfulness of whose earnings he could rely. This is a later form of the practice when pious men had refused the gifts of caliphs because they feared that the money had been acquired unlawfully (by extortion is the technical term). There was always the danger that a tax-gatherer had forced someone to pay more than he ought. If the site of a mosque had been obtained by illegal means, prayer in it was not valid. Here is another example of the lengths to which some went. A man was particular that nothing unclean was eaten in his house. It chanced that his wife was busy when his infant son began to cry; to quiet him a young neighbour who was present gave him the breast. At that moment the father came in. He snatched the child from the self-constituted nurse and held him head downwards that any milk he had swallowed might run out of him. The father feared that the milk might be morally tainted because the woman might have eaten food which did not come up to his standard. The boy grew up with an impediment in his speech which he ascribed to this treatment.

Needless to say such people were aggressively self-righteous and a nuisance to others. Common sense laid down this rule; if you are particular about the purity of food, do not accept an invitation to eat in another's house; but if you accept, eat what is set before you, asking no questions. Muslims may eat the food of Christians and Jews but not that of Magians or idolaters.

Hospitality was one of the chief virtues in pagan Arabia and it was taken over into Islam. Till recently it was everywhere the duty and privilege of the chief of the tribe or the headman of the village to shelter and feed the traveller. With the arrival of hotels the old order has changed. A few quotations will be enough.

> If guests do not enter a house, angels do not enter it.
>
> The humbug, when a guest, talks of the hospitality of Abraham, when a host, of the asceticism of Jesus. Haste is of the devil except in five actions, feeding a guest on his arrival, burying the dead, giving a virgin in marriage, paying a debt, and repenting of sin.

Marriage. A marriage broker, usually an old woman who has access to the women's quarters, is often employed to find out what marriageable girls are available. The first steps are taken by the man's family; it is the custom to get a friend to approach the father of the girl; if it is felt that the families are well matched socially, negotiations can begin in earnest. The essentials of marriage are the presence of witnesses and a contract specifying the *mahr*, bride-price, money or goods given by the groom or his father to the father of the bride. This is a survival of marriage by purchase though the purchase idea was dead when Islam began or even earlier. The *mahr* varies according to the social standing of the parties and national customs; among the bedouin of Sinai it is from one to five camels, four hundred piastres in another tribe, and twenty thousand rupees in a well-to-do Indian family. Then there are individual peculiarities; in an Indian family the *mahr* always includes one gold coin called an ashrafi. The father is expected to spend the money thus received on fitting out his daughter. As a rule only part of the bride-price is paid down; the remainder is paid if the marriage is dissolved. Girls are usually married early but the father or guardian is supposed to ask their consent. The *mahr* is higher for a virgin than for a woman who has been married before. During the wedding festivities the women guests appear unveiled before the bridegroom but it is not etiquette for him to look at them, he must keep his eyes downcast. Local variations in wedding customs are many.

The law allows a man four wives at once but stipulates that he must treat them with equal favour. He may not have two sisters to wife at the same time. He may also have as many concubines as he can afford; a prominent Turk about 1700 exercised this right in Constantinople and was despised for so doing. Social changes in the recent past have had unexpected effects; young men of Jerusalem often go to Syria for their wives because there they can see them before marriage.

Divorce is easy for the man; he has only to pronounce one of the recognized formulae and the divorce is complete. He can however change his mind and take back his wife; if he does not, he must pay up the *mahr* in full. After the lapse of three months she is free to marry again. If the husband wishes a final divorce, he repeats the formula thrice and then he can only remarry the woman after she has been married to another man and the marriage consummated. This was a stock subject for literature. In practice she was married to a slave and then he was given to her; this dissolved the marriage for no woman can own her husband. It is possible for a woman to divorce her husband but in many cases she can only get his consent by renouncing her right to the *mahr*. In law a wife has control of her own property; what happens in actual life will depend on the characters of husband and wife.

The prohibited degrees are much the same as with the Jews. A man may not take his own slave to wife; if he wants to marry her, he must first set her free.

The son of the father's brother has the first claim on a girl's hand; when his right has been ignored, it has happened that he killed the man to whom the girl had been married.

The letter of the law is that no woman may let her face be seen by a man whom it would be lawful for her to marry, one outside the prohibited degrees. Hence the harem and, out-of-doors, the veil. The form of the veil varies from land to land. In Egypt, Syria and Persia among the upper and middle classes it has practically disappeared though elsewhere it still persists. Egyptian divines objected to their present queen showing herself in public unveiled.

A Muslim man may marry a Christian or a Jewess but not an idolater; a Muslim woman may marry none but a Muslim. Were the husband of a Muslim woman to be converted to another religion, the marriage would be dissolved automatically. *Shighār* marriage is forbidden; in this form a man contracted to take another's daughter in marriage, giving his own in return, without any other valuable consideration as *mahr* being demanded by either father, the persons of the wives being considered as *mahr*. This arrangement is legal if a separate *mahr* is provided for each wife. Milk relationship is a bar to marriage; the prohibited degrees are the same through the foster-mother as through the mother.

Among the Malays orthodox ideas on marriage have been powerless in face of old established custom for the freedom of women in this matriarchal land goes back to days before Islam. Exogamous tribes consider many Muslim marriages incestuous though they believe themselves to be good Muslims.

In temporary (*mut'a*) marriage as practised by the Shī'a the bride-price and duration are specified but no expression may be used which implies that the woman is given into the possession of the man for a valuable consideration or as a gift or for hire. The children are legitimate and inherit from the father but the woman has no claim to maintenance and does not inherit from the man. Respectable persons will only enter into such a contract for a term of ninety-nine years.

Circumcision is not mentioned in the Koran but it was adopted by Muḥammad from paganism without question. The school of Mālik calls it commendable but that of Shāfi'ī makes it a duty and the neglect of it punishable. The pious 'Umar II did not demand it from converts. Normally it is regarded as part of Islam, or of the natural religion into which a man is born, or one of the rites of the religion of Abraham. As he is known from tradition to have been circumcised, every good Muslim should copy him. The operation is usually performed at the age of four or later; some even say that the uncircumcised is an unbeliever. In parts of South Arabia a particularly savage form of the rite is the custom as a preliminary to marriage. In some parts the circumcision of women is customary.

The true Malay wedding ceremonies lie outside Muslim law, the henna-staining festivity, the bridegroom's procession, the mimic fights, the ceremonial ablutions of the newly married pair. A wedding before the religious authorities is like a marriage before the registrar; it is tolerated only. A Malay would consider that his daughter had disgraced herself if she was satisfied with a marriage before the local Muslim judge. In Malaya where men emigrate in search of a living or go on pilgrimage to Mecca, the wife has to be safeguarded so a husband may be required immediately after the marriage to pronounce a provisional divorce in such terms as these, "If I am absent for six months and you get no news of me, you are divorced". There is also a divorce by mutual consent when an arbitrator is called in to decide what is to be done; technically this is an ordinary divorce by the husband but he does not have to pay the balance of the bride-price in full. In practice an ill-assorted marriage is only dissolved after much family discussion and with the full knowledge of the Muslim judge, who listens to both parties and tells them what to do and how much they will have to pay or receive.

Adultery. A charge of adultery has to be supported by the evidence of four witnesses and this evidence it is practically impossible to obtain. Two penalties are named in the Koran; in one a hundred strokes for both parties, the other, which mentions only the women, says that they are to be 'kept in houses' till they die. The lawyers divide offenders into two classes, chaste and unchaste. The former are free men and women of full age and understanding who are in a position to enjoy lawful wedlock. The penalty for these is death by stoning. For other persons the penalty is one hundred strokes, fifty if the offender is a slave and banishment for a year, six months for a slave. Lawyers seem to have felt that the basis of this division was unsatisfactory.

A husband, who charges his wife with adultery and cannot bring witnesses, may swear four times that he speaks the truth "and the fifth testimony shall be that the curse of God shall be on him if he be of those who lie". The woman may rebut the charge by a similar oath but the marriage is annulled in perpetuity. This procedure is *liʿān*.

The husband may slay the adulterer without being liable to retaliation. In practice the relatives of the guilty woman pay no heed to the law but kill her; drowning is the favourite form of the punishment. Fornication is forbidden for chastity is the duty of the believer. This part of the law is often forgotten. Rape is a form of unchastity coupled with injury to the person.

It is curious that Semitic languages have one word to express all sexual offences.

Adoption. In pagan Arabia adoption conferred all the privileges and duties of birth. Muḥammad adopted a son who was thenceforward known as son of Muḥammad. One day he saw this son's wife and was attracted by her. Her husband divorced her and Muḥammad married her. To stop the scandal he received a revelation that an adopted son was to be known by the name of his real father. The Ḥanafī school interprets this to mean that adopted sons (daughters are not mentioned) have no right of inheritance and none of the duties of true children. Adoption of children is free to any man of full age and to any woman who has her husband's consent. If one or both of the parents are known there is no legal obligation on the adoptive parents to support the child though moral obligation remains. The Mālikī school permits the adopted child to inherit from its new parents but restricts adoption to those who would not otherwise be entitled to share in the inheritance. It seems that the object of this restriction is to prevent a man favouring one relative at the expense of others. Among the nomads of Moab full adoption can take place but, as the admission of an outsider concerns the tribe as well as the family, the assent of the chief is necessary.

'Aqīqa ceremony. On the seventh day after the birth it is commendable to name the child, cut its hair, and offer a sacrifice, two sheep or goats for a boy, one for a girl. If not made at this time, the sacrifice can be made later, even by the child itself when grown-up. The flesh should be given to the poor. The weight of the hair in silver or gold should be distributed in alms. The Ẓāhiri school made this ceremony a duty. The Arab nomads now offer one animal for a boy but none for a girl. The sacrifice and the shorn hair are both called *'aqīqa.* The custom is clearly a survival from pagan times.

Death and *Burial.* When death occurs, the body is washed (normally by persons of the same sex) an uneven number of times with water in which the leaves of the lote tree have been soaked. The orifices of the body are plugged and the grave clothes put on. A pious man will often have his grave clothes ready and, if he has made the pilgrimage, will have brought them from Mecca. Burial follows death quickly. Short prayers are said over the dead without bowing or prostration and usually not in a mosque. The body is carried at a smart pace on an open bier covered with a shroud. Coffins are not used except when a body is exhumed to be transferred to another grave. The grave is so arranged that the earth does not press on the body; there is either a trench in the floor of the pit or a niche at the side; the trench is covered with flat stones and the niche walled off. The corpse is laid on its right side with the face towards Mecca. The grave should be level with the ground. A man attended the funeral of a prince of the Abbasid house and noticed four men burying a slave; he said, "I walked away with a friend and we turned back to look at the grave but could not tell which was the grave of the prince and which that of the slave".

A man and a woman are not buried in the same grave and, if this in unavoidable, a partition is put between them.

A common monument is two posts, one at the head and one at the foot, with the name of the deceased and verses from the Koran. When the tomb is covered with a slab of stone, a hole is often left in the middle; the popular explanation in Turkey is that it is for the soul to breathe through. It may be connected with the old custom of sprinkling water on a grave. Elaborate monuments were built over the graves of important people but they vary from country to country; as a rule, a mosque which has a dome, is also a tomb.

The women of the family visit the grave on the Friday after the funeral generally taking a palm branch to break up and place on the grave and some cakes or bread to distribute to the poor. This is repeated in the two following weeks and on the Friday which completes or next follows the period of forty days after the funeral. It is not good to lament and cry by the grave for, indeed, the dead suffer as do the living. The tale is told that a tutor died and his charges visited his tomb on the sixth day, talking about him, eating figs and throwing the stalks on the grave. He appeared to their father in a dream and complained that the boys had made a dust heap of his grave.

A cemetery, which is honoured by having the tomb of a saint, is a favourite place for burial, the nearer the saint the better to be sure of his protection; proximity is also more expensive. Many Persians wish to be buried at the Shī'a shrines of Najaf and Karbala so many caravans brought corpses to these places. The bodies were enclosed in coffins.

Slavery. Like all old civilizations Islam takes slavery for granted. English readers must be told to forget all about *Uncle Tom's Cabin* and the ideas associated with it; indeed a modern traveller has said, "I have met slaves who would be the better for a little cruelty, say every Saturday night". Slaves were employed in the house, the garden, or the fields but there was no exploitation of slave labour on a large scale. Religion enjoined men to treat their slaves kindly and to give them the same clothes and food as the masters used. It was a pious act to set free a slave, it was often done at death and the manumission of a slave or slaves was the atonement for certain ritual offences.

During the conquests many prisoners of war became slaves and descendants of these are among the great names of Islam. Ḥasan of Basra was one of them; in books on religion the name Ḥasan without any qualification refers to this man. When a man had a young son, it was common to buy a boy of the same age as a companion for him; the two grew up together and the slave was the trusted and trustworthy friend of his master. Some male slaves served in the women's quarters and in India today elderly men, who have spent their lives in the services of the family, take the place of slaves. A woman was nurse to several generations of a family and one of her charges, when himself a father, addressed her as 'mother'; it is not definitely stated that she was a slave but this is the natural assumption.

Muḥammad 'Alī, the viceroy of Egypt, was seated cross-legged giving audience to a European when he complained to the slave behind him that he could not find his handkerchief. The slave rolled the pasha over on to his side, felt in the pocket of the baggy trousers and finally produced the missing handkerchief. Then he set his master right way up again. The audience was in no way interrupted. There is no need to point the moral.

'Umar I ruled that an Arab could not be a slave. The law forbids a Muslim to enslave a fellow Muslim but the conversion of a slave does not set him free. It is forbidden to parents to sell their children as slaves but it has happened. In a Muslim state Jews and Christians are not allowed to own Muslim slaves; if a slave of one of them turns Muslim, he must be sold to a Muslim. From some aspects a slave is only half a man; he cannot have more than two wives and for offences the penalty for a slave is half that for a free man, forty stripes instead of eighty for drunkenness. A slave cannot be a witness and cannot hold property; whatever he has belongs to his master so, if he is killed, the blood money is paid to his owner. He can be an agent for his master and as such make contracts in his name. One trader had several slaves each of whom had 100,000 dinars at his disposal for trade. There were two special classes of slaves; those to whom their masters had promised freedom at their death and those who had been allowed to contract to purchase their freedom out of the profits of their industry.

A man may not marry his own slave; if he wishes to do so, he must first set her free. (See above: *Marriage*.)

If a woman bears a child to her owner, she cannot be sold and becomes free at the owner's death. If a man marries another's slave, the children are slaves and belong to the owner of their mother. A man is permitted women from the people of the book as concubines but not idolaters. The children of a concubine rank with those of a free woman as heirs. Amīn the son of Hārūn Rashīd was the son of an Arab woman and so took precedence over his half-brother Ma'mūn because he was the son of a slave; this was a relic of Arab pride. Later the law came to be respected.

Another class of slaves were the mamlukes; the word means 'owned', was at first applied to any slave, then later was restricted to those who were bought to be trained as soldiers. When these men made themselves rulers of Egypt, they formed the aristocracy and no one was thought worthy of occupying the throne unless he had first been a slave.

Many of the famous women singers were slaves; they were carefully trained, fetched high prices, and gave themselves all the airs of a film star. There is a tale of a man who savagely flogged a slave girl but, by so doing, he put himself outside the pale of decent folk.

If a freed man died without heirs, his former owner or his heirs inherited the property.

Trade. Here the difference between the law and the practice of the community is wide. The law forbids the sale of certain goods, such as dogs, pigs, wine and (ritually) unclean olives because they are unclean or unfit for human consumption. The purchase of grape juice from one who makes wine or of any goods from one whose property has been unlawfully acquired is not approved though it is not forbidden. It is illegal to sell anything not yet in existence such as the fruit of an orchard or a crop before they are ripe. A sale must be completed and delivery taken within three days of making the contract. The purchaser only takes possession with the delivery of the goods and till then the seller is responsible; if the buyer dies before taking delivery the sale is void. It is illegal to sell what cannot be delivered, e.g. a runaway slave, and any goods of which the exact quantity is unknown, e.g. a heap of grain. The object of other restrictions appears to be the prevention of speculation. Some say that it is lawful to buy goods which have not been seen if an exact specification has been given and the buyer has the right of rejection if they do not agree with the description. Speaking generally a sale is invalid if conditions are attached to it; unless they are essential like the stipulation that a garden must be watered regularly. A teacher of the Koran may agree to be paid when the pupil has learnt it by heart and a doctor if and when the cure has been effected.

It is lawful to sell goods at a profit if the cost price and the amount of profit are disclosed. It is illegal to sell like for like, gold for gold or dates for dates. The Koran forbids a practice which a commentator describes as buying some foodstuff for a fixed period and returning it (in larger quantity) after the term. It is, he says, like paying two dirhams for one and who will buy goods worth two dirhams for one unless pressed by need or hoping for profit! This prohibition is applied by the commentators to gold, silver and food while tradition limits the food to wheat, barley, dates and raisins. This is the base for the prohibition of interest.

Trade has been carried on according to local custom and various devices have been invented to circumvent the law. A common trick is for the borrower to sell something, valuable or not, to the lender and to buy it back at an enhanced price. In Egypt Muḥammad 'Abduh, in his capacity as muftī, gave a ruling that the interest allowed by the post office savings bank was lawful and this rule has been followed elsewhere. In India this bank has lakhs of rupees of unclaimed interest due to pious Muslims.

The sale of an unclean thing may be avoided by a formula which confers the right to use it. To avoid the three days' rule the buyer makes an advance payment to secure an option on the goods which he can refuse if they are not up to specification. In business not much importance attaches to written documents. A contract is usually verbal; Shāfi'ī says that such a contract is binding as soon as the two parties have gone their separate ways; Mālik says, as soon as it is concluded.

Most men wear a seal ring set with a semi-precious stone on which is engraved the owner's name; the ring is silver for the prophet disapproved of gold ornaments for men. The seal impression is more important than the signature; anyone can write a man's name but only one should have his seal.

Music. There was great debate about the lawfulness of music; traditions were quoted on both sides. This tale is instructive. One afternoon in Medina a man was singing as he walked along. A head came out of a window above him and a voice said, "You are doing three wrong things, you are singing, you are disturbing folk's siesta, and you are singing out of tune." The voice sang the song correctly, and said, "When young I was fond of music but mother told me that I was not good-looking enough to make a success of it and advised me to study law." It is alleged that the speaker was Mālik. The law is against music in every form; it is never used in the worship of the mosque and those, who wish to appear righteous are ostentatious in their avoidance of it. Objection was taken to music because it was usually accompanied by wine and women. Others heard and hear it gladly and do not bother about the frown of authority. Mystics used it to induce the ecstasy in which communion with God becomes easier. Literature is full of the emotional power of it; men swooned and even fell dead on hearing a song which harmonized with their mood of the moment. Ghazālī has a long discussion on music and concludes that it is a valuable aid to worship though it can be dangerous and so its use must be hedged about with restrictions. Danger may lie in the performer, the instrument, the song, and the listener. The performer must not be a woman of the prohibited degrees, nor the instruments those used to accompany drinking, nor the songs immoral or irreligious, nor the hearers be young and without the love of God.

Painting and sculpture. Muḥammad said that anyone who made a representation of any living thing would be called on at the judgement to give life to what he had made and would be covered with shame because he would fail to do so. Therefore orthodox opinion condemns both painting and sculpture though some are less severe on painting. One result was the development of geometrical and arabesque ornament and of Arabic calligraphy; a choice specimen of writing is often a prominent decoration in a room. A frieze of inscriptions was a common adornment of a building. The prohibition was often flouted. Trees figure in the mosaics of the mosque of Damascus which were the work of Byzantine craftsmen and the human form is painted on the walls of Qusair 'Amr, the Umayyad hunting lodge. Pictures, some obscene, were common in baths. The Persians pictured animals and men on carpets, metal, pottery and paper; there is no need to praise the grace and splendour of their miniatures. The Indians followed them in painting. A few Arabic manuscripts have pictures. Historians tell of fountains in animal form in Spain. Perhaps the lions in the Alhambra are a deliberate refusal to copy nature too closely. Korans and mosques were never adorned with figures. Today photographs are common, many newspapers are illustrated and statues are erected to famous men.

Apostasy. Death is the penalty for apostasy though some say that the offender must be given the opportunity to repent and the penalty is to be inflicted only when he is obdurate. When the Almohades captured Cordoba the Jews and Christians were banished, among them the family of Maimonides. It is said that these last in the course of their wanderings pretended to be Muslims. In Cairo Maimonides was accused of being a pervert but the judge refused to condemn him on the ground that 'forced conversion is no conversion'. This tale has been rejected as unhistorical because no judge would go against the letter of the law; Muslims however found it possible to believe it. About the year 1300 it was discovered that Buddhist monks, who had been converted when their temples were destroyed, had only made a pretence of being converted so they were given permission to go to Tibet, if they wished, where they would be free to follow their real faith. In the seventeenth century the governor of Ispahan forced some Jews to turn Muslim but the Shah intervened and "suffered them to resume their own religion and live in quiet". The law was merciful to one who denied his religion to save his life.

The Universe. The created universe contains the throne of God, heaven, paradise, earth and hell. There are seven heavens, seven earths and seven hells. Compared to the throne the highest heaven is like a ring tossed into a desert. On his night journey Muḥammad passed through the heavens meeting Adam in the first, in the second Jesus and Yaḥyā (John the Baptist), in the third Joseph, in the fourth Idrīs, in the fifth Aaron, in the sixth Moses, and in the seventh Abraham. All souls are paraded before Adam in the first heaven. This scheme does not agree with the belief that all the blessed pass into paradise which is beyond the heavens. The Koran has several names for paradise, *firdaws*, the garden, the garden of 'Adn. This last is obviously the garden of Eden but Muslims explain the name from Arabic as 'the permanent garden'. It is argued that the paradise of the blessed is not that from which Adam was expelled for no one is ever driven out of it.

This earth is the highest of the seven; the lowest is supported by a bull and that by a fish beneath which is hell. The habitable world is divided into seven parallel climes or zones, all north of the equator. Negroes live in the southernmost and the inhabitants of the other zones become progressively lighter in colour till the uninhabitable north is reached.

Hell is usually pictured as a pit with seven storeys. In the lowest are the roots of the tree Zaqqūm which reaches to the top of hell with its fruits of demons' heads. Torments include intense cold and intense heat; when the skins of the wicked have been burnt off, new ones grow that the torment may be renewed. Hell is also pictured as a monstrous animal. When God gives the order to fetch hell, it trembles and needs to be reassured by angels that He will not punish it. It has four feet and each foot is fettered by 70,000 rings on each of which sit 70,000 demons.

Mecca is the navel of the earth; it was created first and round it the world spread out; it is the highest point, the spot from which the world draws its nutriment and it is the junction with the upper and lower worlds. So it is called 'the mother of towns'. The site of the Ka'ba corresponds to that of the pole star. Ishmael and hundreds of prophets are buried round it. It is the centre of the universe; its foundation is in the lowest earth and forms an axis which passes through the whole seven. Each stage in the universe has its sanctuary; the throne of God is the highest. Two others in the heavens are known by name, the *bait ma'mūr* and *ḍurāḥ*. Another report says that these are two names for one place; it is the counterpart in heaven of the Ka'ba on earth.

Saints. A reputation as a saint may be got in many ways; by miracles, ecstasy, hereditary holiness, charity, asceticism, mendiancy, the foundation of a dervish order, or even lunacy. Saints receive their power from God, do not acquire it by their own merits. The hierarchy of the saints is much the same as that of the mystics. Some are revered throughout the world while others are local. Some are obviously pre-Islamic objects of worship, especially those connected with sacred trees, springs, and caves which have been converted to serve Muslim purposes. The power of a saint is called *baraka*, blessing, and this is imagined as almost tangible. By kissing the saint's hand or tomb, this power passes to the worshipper who will be helped by it. Like all holy things it may be dangerous to those who would misuse it. Orthodoxy recognizes saints who work wonders; these are not called miracles but charismatic gifts. Of course, it is not the man who works but God who works through him, A common form of praise is "his prayers were answered", in other words, he could be relied on to get from God what he asked. Sainthood endured after death so worship at shrines became popular in spite of the opposition of the rigorists.

No one dares to violate the sanctity of a saint's tomb so anything left under his protection is safe. The peasant leaves his plough there, secure that none will touch it. A hunter saw a gazelle by a heap of stones, fired and missed. The man suddenly felt drowsy and fell asleep; when he awoke, he was conscious that something had happened to him. He had turned into a woman! He went home and had difficulty in making himself known to his people. A wise man was fetched who solved the problem. The heap of stones was a tomb and the saint had shown his anger at the presumptuous man who had ignored his protection by firing at the gazelle. A sacrifice was offered, the man went to sleep again, and woke in his proper form. It happens that a man will swear falsely by God, for He is far away, but he dare not swear falsely by the local or tribal saint, for he is near and touchy. A woman in North Africa let her baby fall into a well and called on 'Abd al-Qādir to save it. A local 'Abd al-Qādir caught the infant half-way down the pit but the great 'Abd al-Qādir from Baghdad, who arrived at the bottom a fraction of a second later, was annoyed to find that his journey had been wasted.

Usually a saint has an annual festival. In Egypt this is called *mawlid*, birthday, and is very popular; there may be a procession, prayers in the mosque, and a fair; all tastes are catered for and all enjoy themselves. An historian tells of a mosque tomb in Egypt at which folk made vows and to which they brought their troubles, requests for payment of debts, the gift of children, and such-like though they should have asked them from God alone. He then proved that the saint could not have been buried there and adds that the tomb was just like the sacred stones to which the pagan Arabs turned in trouble. An irreverent tale laughs at the respect for saints by telling how a donkey and its foal came to be honoured with shrines to which the faithful brought their offerings.

Closely connected with saints are the *sayyids* and *sharīfs*. It has already been said that there is no aristocracy in Islam; that statement requires some qualification for the descendants of the prophet occupy a privileged position. It is usually said that a sayyid is a descendant of Ḥasan and a sharif a descendant of Ḥusain, the two grandsons of the prophet, but this is not always right. In South Arabia *sharīfa* is the feminine of *sayyid*. In the Middle Ages in every great city one of the family was an official (*naqīb*) whose duty it was to watch over the titles and ensure that no spurious claims were admitted. A few years back the *naqīb* was a man of great influence in Baghdad and was head of one of the first governments after the expulsion of the Turks. In South Arabia the *sayyids* do not carry arms (there are exceptions) and hold a position above the warring tribes which enables them to act as arbitrators and peacemakers. In Morocco some of them, like the Sharif of Wazzan, are saints and are almost worshipped. There are also whole tribes of sharifs, real and so-called. Arab warriors of the group Ma'qil conquered the Berber Zenāga; the only counterpoise these could offer to the military nobility of the Arabs was to turn themselves into a tribe of sharifs. What men thought of some of these aristocrats is shown by the Indian saying, "I was a weaver (by caste); this year I am a shaikh; and next year, if the harvest be good, I shall be a *sayyid*".

In South Arabia are persons and clans called *mashāïkh* (the plural of shaikh) who are usually descendants of local saints and so are natives of the country as opposed to the *sharifs* who, if genuine, must be immigrants. The holiness of their ancestor still clings to them and gives them great religious influence.

In Morocco a holy man is a marabut, a corruption of *murābiṭ* which originally meant a soldier in the holy war. There are whole tribes of them who are often appealed to as arbitrators and their influence has been on the whole pacific. Like the religious orders they have their convents which dispense hospitality and instruction. In the Rio de Oro the marabut tribes stand nominally next in consideration after the warrior tribes and are more peaceful, devoting themselves to trade and camel breeding. Generally they are under the protection of a warrior tribe to whom they pay the 'brotherhood' tax, in other words, blackmail.

In India Khaḍir is connected with water and is invoked when there is too much or too little, in drought and flood. He rides on a fish which became the arms of the rulers of Oudh. He has no shrines but it is customary to make little rafts carrying a lamp, flowers and sweetmeats and set them adrift on the river at the end of the rains.

Many shrines have the right of asylum; in Fez alone there were thirty-eight though the French have abolished all of them except the great mosque. In Hadramaut a village of *sayyids* "was the scene of an annual fair at which, if you reached it without being shot at, you were safe, for the place was a sanctuary".

Oaths and vows. The Koran deprecates the use of oaths in ordinary talk, they should be reserved for serious matters. If a man breaks an oath, he can offer atonement by feeding or clothing ten poor men, manumitting a slave or, if he is poor, fasting for three consecutive days. A tradition says that there is no wrong in breaking an oath if a better course of action presents itself. A weighty oath was, "to divorce my wives, set free my slaves and give my property in alms". The ease with which an oath could be set aside led to a disregard for its sanctity. If a man has sworn in error and finds that what he believed to be true is not so, there is no need for expiation; but if he knew that he swore falsely, there can be no expiation, he can only repent and hope for God's mercy. Mālik ruled that if a man swore to give all his property in alms, it was enough to give one-third. He also ruled that, if he swore to sacrifice his son at the station of Abraham, he must sacrifice a sheep at Mecca, but if the station was not named, he was not liable for anything. A vow to pray in the mosque of Mecca, Medina or Jerusalem should be kept to the letter; but if any other mosque was named, the man might keep his vow by praying wherever he happened to be. A vow to do what is wrong need not be kept.

Oaths and vows should be made in the name of God, neither the prophet, the Ka'ba nor any other sanctity should be invoked. Actually an oath by the local saint is more likely to be valuable; the saint is close at hand and jealous of his honour while God is far off. In early times a vow or oath made at the time of the afternoon prayer was specially binding.

Among the marsh Arabs of Iraq, 'Abbās, the son of 'Alī by a bedouin woman, he, who according to tradition lost both arms and finally his life in an endeavour to fetch water for Ḥusain on the fatal day of Karbala, is known among the tribes as the Father of the Hot Head, and is famed for the swiftness of his vengeance. An oath by the 'flag of 'Abbās' is the most potent of all. A piece of reed as tall as a man is taken, "the sword of '*Abbās*" and a white cloth is tied to it, "the flag of God, of Muḥammad His prophet and of 'Alī and its avenger is 'Abbās, the man with the hot head". Each man who has to swear ties a knot in the cloth round the reed. The first man says, "This flag is on me, on my eyes and on my life, on my brothers, and on my kindred. Nothing is concealed nor hidden, and its avenger is 'Abbās". Those who follow say, "I tie this flag on me, on my brothers and on my kindred". Breach of this oath will be followed by punishment swiftly and surely.

Sacrifice. Sacrifices are frequently offered on the day the pilgrims make their offerings at Mina.

In Morocco if a man wants the help of another he puts on him '*ār* (shame); this can be done in many ways but a powerful method is to slaughter an animal at the door of his house or the entrance to his tent. If the man steps over the blood or even sees it, he accepts the implied obligation. If he has not seen the blood, he can tell his servants to wash it away and to remove the carcase; then he is under no obligation to the suppliant. This is a survival of an old custom as similar sacrifices are recorded from South Arabia.

In Moab sacrifices are offered to 'the face of God' in time of danger, as at the threat of an epidemic. One form of the rite is for each family to cut its offering in two, hang the halves on posts and the family will then march between them. A sacrifice to a saint must be left for the poor. When a man cannot afford an animal he may smear butter or oil on the tomb.

On the day when the sacrifices are offered at Mina it is customary to offer a sacrifice, in Iraq a cow, for those of the family who have died during the year. The bedouin offer a camel for each individual. In India the Muslims often provoked trouble by parading the decorated cow through the Hindu quarters of the town.

Magic. Belief in magic is closely connected with that in jinn. Three kinds of acts violate the order of nature, Muslims say, violate custom. The miracles of prophets, wonders wrought by saints, and magical acts. A prophet works miracles to prove his mission and summons his opponents to do the like—a challenge which they fail to meet. Wonders proceed from saints without any exertion on their part and are accompanied by no such challenge. Magical acts are the result of labour and long practice. Were a magician to claim that his wonders were a proof of his being a prophet, he would fail to produce them. The miracles of saints and prophets come from God; the works of magic from the jinn.

In Arabia before Islam soothsayers, magicians, and poets were all under the influence of jinn. These went as close to heaven as they dared to overhear the heavenly counsels; what they heard they repeated to the soothsayers. Sometimes they did not hear distinctly. Shooting stars are missiles hurled by angels at these intruders to drive them off. With the mission of Muḥammad the heavenly guards became more alert. A poet boasted to a rival that he was more prolific. The rival answered, "you take everything which your jinn gives you; I am critical of what mine brings me".

Magic may be white or black, licit or illicit. The white is formed by the help of God; Solomon was the first great practitioner of it. Persians give this place to Jamshid. Black is worked by men who have learned to compel jinn and demons to serve them; it began with the daughter of Iblīs. Magic may be worked by the power of the soul or by material objects, amulets or talismans. Verses from the Koran, especially the last two chapters, "the two apotropaics", and magic squares are very common. Belief in the evil eye is almost universal. Some limit the power of magic to causing enmity between a man and his wife but orthodoxy says it can do more than this.

Opinions differ on the lawfulness of magic; here follow examples. It is forbidden both to teach and to learn it; it is forbidden to teach it if this will lead to sin; it is allowed to teach it to ward off the magic of a wicked man. Shāfi'ī held that a sorcerer is not an unbeliever unless his acts are, for other reasons, those of an unbeliever.

It may be noted that the jinn are sometimes very stupid. When Solomon died he was buried standing, leaning on a staff. The jinn, who served him, did not know that he was dead till white ants gnawed through the staff and the corpse fell down.

A parallel is drawn between men and jinn; soothsayers are apostles of the jinn, tattooing their books, lies their traditions, poetry their religious recitations, the flute their muezzin, the market their mosque, baths their home, their food what has not had the name of God invoked over it, their drink intoxicating liquor, and their hunting ground women.

A common form of magic is the *zār*. The usual word for mad means possessed by jinn. Belief in possession and proceedings to remove it are current in the Sudan, Egypt, and Mecca whence they have spread to Oman; the occurrence of the *zār* in Egypt was first noticed in print in Egypt in 1885. The practices arose in Central Africa or Abyssinia and travelled northwards; they are not known in Syria. *Zār* denotes both the spirit and the ritual. The exorcist is of the same sex as the patient and is accompanied by an orchestra for the spirit is expelled by music. With a new patient the exorcist has to find out the place of origin and the name of the spirit for these determine the colours of the clothes to be worn and the tune which will drive it out. When the right melody has been found, a matter of trial and error, the singing may go on all night culminating in the sacrifice of a fowl. This seems to be the original offering though sometimes a sheep is substituted and occasionally both are offered. If the patient is rich the incantations may go on for as many as seven nights. For those who cannot afford such extravagance, the ceremony is held regularly at certain shrines. A sacrifice does not always occur; several women may dance, apparently in some kind of trance; sometimes, at any rate, the chief patient neither dances nor falls into a trance. One man declared that he felt seriously ill if he did not attend a *zār* every two or three weeks. It seems that these practices are widespread in all classes of society in Egypt. In Morocco the Gnawa, a fraternity consisting chiefly of negroes, are experts in expelling jinn from those troubled by them. Their performance is very like the *zār*.

Dreams. Messages from the unseen world are received in dreams; this belief is crystallized in a tradition, "dreams are one forty-sixth part of prophecy". In sleep when sensations from outside the body are not perceived at all or only weakly, the mind is free to attend to messages from the upper world.

One writer divides dreams into three classes, those sent by God which are self-explanatory and do not need interpretation, those sent by angels which have to be interpreted, and those sent by demons which are nightmares. In another place he ascribes nightmares to disturbances in the body. Truthful dreams may give information about something already existing, such as the whereabouts of a hidden treasure, or foretell something that is going to happen. As a man can think only along the lines of his experience, when an idea is given in sleep, the imagination seizes it, clothes it in some familiar form that suits it, so the resultant dream needs an interpreter. Many books were written on this subject and it is common to find in the biographical dictionaries scholars who were famous as interpreters of dreams. Apparently there is no certain way of deciding whether a dream is truthful or not.

The Next World. It has already been noticed that official descriptions of the hereafter are inconsistent; the scales, the books, and the bridge are separate and mutually exclusive accounts of the last judgement. Popular ideas are even more confused. In the grave the works of a good man appear to him in a beautiful form and those of a bad man in a terrifying shape. A bad man's works also appear as a dog which tortures him in the measure of his guilt or in the shape of a young pig.

There was much uncertainty as to the abode of the dead between death and the judgement. Some put them in *barzakh*. In the Koran *barzakh* is a division between heaven and hell; a commentator insists that it is a moral barrier. It is defined as 'what is between this world and the next from death till the resurrection', 'what is between the dead and return to this world', and 'what is after death' Entrance into *barzakh* is a euphemism for death. Not every one entered *barzakh* which might be a place of punishment. One account divides the dead into classes. The bodies of some turn to dust and their souls wander in the world of sovereignty (*malakūt*) under the sky of this world. Some sleep and know nothing till the first trump wakes them; then they die (the second death). Some remain two or three months in the grave and then their souls fly on birds to paradise. Some ascend to the trump and stay close to it till it sounds; there are as many recesses in it as there are souls.

Prophets and saints have the choice of remaining in this world and appearing to men in dreams or of ascending to one of the heavens. Muḥammad stayed on the earth for thirty years till the murder of Ḥusain when he ascended to heaven in disgust. A Wahhābī believed that Muḥammad was alive in his grave like other prophets with more life than the martyrs.

According to a mystical interpretation the perfect man is *barzakh*, an intermediary between God and the universe in the sense of being the only creature which unites and manifests both perfectly.

The dead, who wander in the earth, surround the dying when they are at the last gasp and fill the house till it cannot contain them. When a dead man arrives from the earth, they crowd round the new-comer asking news of their friends.

At the last earth and heaven are violently shaken and are emptied of their inhabitants. A fire comes out from hell and burns till the earth is a black cinder and the skies boiling oil; then it is sent back to hell. The water of life descends from the throne of God, moistens the earth and the dead come back to life. God restores Isrāfīl to life and he sounds the first trump when all souls return to their bodies. True believers, who died during the pilgrimage, will be given garments from paradise. In the interval between the two blasts of the trump will be the second death; the interval is said to be forty years. At this point all are seated on their graves. The deeds of good men become animals, camels, mules, asses, on which they ride to the scene of judgement. There they will be tormented with thirst and boys will give cold water to fathers whose sons have died. This is the advantage of marriage. Hell escapes from its guardians and swoops down on the assembly till even apostles are afraid.

Some stories represent God as an Oriental potentate whose anger can be turned away by an apt answer. Thus God said, "O wicked old man, you have done this evil and that". The man replied, "What am I to think of tradition which says that God proclaimed that He would be ashamed to torture one who had grown old in Islam?" God smiled and said, "What you, the narrators of the tradition, and I have said is true. Go; I pardon you".

An entirely different set of beliefs about the hereafter is indicated by the statement that the spirits of believers are in Jabia in Syria and those of unbelievers in Barhūt in Hadramaut; one version says, in a salt swamp in Hadramaut. Unbelievers are also said to be in Sijjīn in the seventh earth.

In paradise the waste products from the bodies of the blessed are eliminated in the form of sweat. Crude ideas still persist in out of the way places. A medical missionary treated a Kurd and, when he refused to take any payment, the grateful patient said, "In paradise I shall have seventy virgins, I shall not want them all. In the place where you are going you will have none; you can have two of mine".

Syncretism. Among simple Muslims, and sometimes among those who are not simple, mixed worship exists. Many Muslim Rajputs employ Brahmans at their marriages and keep a family priest (*purohita*) to read *mantras* on solemn occasions. Many of the working class scrupulously avoid eating or even touching beef, and openly worship and offer vows to Hindu gods; they wear Hindu dress and that in a land where dress is a badge of religion. They seldom visit a mosque and seldom perform any Muslim rites except circumcision. A caste of masons and bricklayers worship their tools at the *'īd al-fiṭr*, offering sweetmeats to them like the Hindus who worship their tools at Dasahra. Muslim missionaries are working to correct this state of things. In many places holy springs and caves are survivals of earlier faiths. Some instances from the former Ottoman empire may be given. During a plague of locusts Muslims and Christians joined their supplications and even shared a procession. In an epidemic of cholera Turks begged that the body of a Greek saint might be carried in parade through the Turkish quarters of the town. The epidemic ceased. Turks frequented a ruined church in Philadelphia because the lighting of a candle in it cured toothache. Muslim women sat under the altar during the celebration of public worship; their own saints had failed them so they tried the Christian. Apparently all saints are powerful and it is well to keep on good terms with them. Muslims frequented the synagogue at Bona on Friday evenings to seek healing, children, or success in their ventures. In Egypt is a survival of another kind where boats are or were carried in the procession at the annual festival of two saints. The festival of Aḥmad al-Badawī at Tanta is held according to the solar calendar. In Morocco one of the chief carnivals is the students' festival at Fez; a prisoner is set free in circumstances which recall the part of Barabbas in the story of the Passion.

Some miscellaneous customs and beliefs may be mentioned here. When a child is born, the call to prayer is whispered into its right ear as a defence against jinn. A pious Muslim will sometimes perform the ritual ablution at the approach of death so that he may die in a state of purity. The face of the dying man is turned towards Mecca and, if possible, he repeats the confession. On the night of the middle of Sha'bān is decided who shall die during the following twelve months. A tree in paradise, 'the *sidra* tree which marks the boundary', as it is called in the Koran, has as many leaves as there are inhabitants in the world and on each leaf a name is written. On this night the tree is shaken and those, whose leaves fall, will die during the year. During the last ten days of Ramaḍān falls the night of power on which the Koran was sent down. On this night the gates of heaven are open so prayers are sure to be heard and answered; angels descend to the earth with blessings and salt water becomes sweet. The prevalent opinion is that the 27th, is the night but this is not certain so, to be on the safe side, some pay the same respect to all the odd nights in the last decade of the month. This is another instance of the respect for odd numbers.

A custom which has now lapsed was the *dawsa* (doseh). On the birthday of the prophet at Cairo a number of dervishes lay face downwards on the ground, as close together as they could, and the head of the order rode on horseback along the path so formed. Men said that both the dervishes and the chief prepared for the ordeal by special prayers. This riding over the bodies of men took place also at the festival of the lady Zainab, the granddaughter of Muḥammad.

'Āshūrā, the tenth day of Muḥarram, is the day on which Adam and Eve met after they had been driven out of the garden, on which Noah came out of the ark, and on which Ḥusain was killed. Muḥammad had fixed this day to be observed as a fast from sunrise to sunset but when he had to give up his hopes of the Jews, the fast of Ramaḍān was instituted and fasting on 'Āshūrā ceased to be obligatory though it was commendable. In modern Egypt a special dish of food is associated with this day. It may be noted that it is wrong to fast on a feast day.

CHAPTER X

MODERN MOVEMENTS

MODERN movements may be modern only in time like the Wahhābī which is nothing but a resurrection of old ideas. This had some influence in the east and started or helped to start religious ferments. These and similar revolts will be taken first and after them the modernist movements, those due to the stirring of new ideas.

In Malaya. At the beginning of the nineteenth century returning pilgrims brought Wahhābī ideas to Central Sumatra where they received the support of prominent leaders of religion. They enforced Muslim law, especially the ceremonial law and tried to put down cock fighting with its attendant betting, the use of dice, palm wine, opium, betel and tobacco, the filing of the teeth and long finger-nails. The men were forced to shave their heads, let their beards grow, and wear white clothes like the Arabs and they compelled the women to be veiled. All these regulations, except the prohibition of tobacco, are part of the code of Shāfi'ī. These reformers were called Padris (Padaries, Pedaries); they tried to break down the local matriarchal system and so were opposed by the chiefs. Supported by the divines the Padris imposed their system by armed force, plundering those who opposed them. Some held that he, who did not observe prayer at the right time, was an apostate to be killed; others held that a first offence was to be punished by a fine and a second offence by death. The movement was suppressed by the Dutch in 1832.

In 1921 a Muslim society in Java affirmed these principles: the influence of European capital in enslaving the natives is dangerous; Islam demands government by the people, workers' councils, the right to work, division of the land and means of production, and forbids men to enrich themselves by the labour of others; and asserted its readiness to join international organizations regardless of the barriers set up by Islam. No wonder the society was called communist. Another society is concerned only with religion and tries to spread the Islam of Muḥammad ʿAbduh, often without mentioning his name.

In Persia at the beginning of the nineteenth century Shaikh Aḥmad of Aḥsā began to teach that the twelve imams were the first of created beings. They are the effective cause of the rest of creation, being the scene of the manifestation of the divine will; had they not existed God could not have created anything for they are the organs of transmission of the acts of deity. God, being incomprehensible, can only be understood through the medium of the imams who are hypostases of the supreme being; to sin against them is to sin against God. The 'preserved tablet' is the heart of the imams. Their material bodies are subject to decay; this is not the Shīʿa doctrine. Man's physical body will not share in the resurrection but he has what may be called an astral body which will be the resurrection body. Later the doctrine of the body was further developed. Man has two *jasad* and two *jism* (both words mean body). The first *jasad* is the physical body which will not be raised again, the second will reappear in the hereafter. The first *jism* will be worn in *barzakh* while the second exists in isolation from death till the first trump when it will be joined with the spirit and the second *jasad* to form the resurrection man.

God's knowledge is twofold. 1. His essential knowledge has no connection with the contingent and phenomenal. 2. His originated knowledge is the actual being of the known; the twelve imams are the doors which give access to it; it is not an attribute of God but is present before Him. It also is twofold, a knowledge of possibility and a knowledge of things. The former is concerned with things before they exist and the second with things after they have come into being.

The world is eternal in time but new in essence for accidents without substance or forms without substratum cannot come into existence. Accidents are transitory novelties but substance is not; therefore matter is a novelty in essence and will have no end though it had a beginning. Were it not so, paradise and hell would come to an end. Both are created by the acts of men. Paradise is love for the family of Muḥammad. Aḥmad condemned the pantheism of the mystics and explained the miracles of Muḥammad symbolically. He hinted that the coming of the hidden imam was at hand.

Though modern in date this movement was thoroughly mediaeval in its ideas.

Bābī. In 1844 Sayyid 'Alī Muḥammad, a pupil of Shaikh Aḥmad of Aḥsā, announced that he was the Bāb (door to knowledge of the truth). Pretending to reform Islam he founded a new religion with its own dogmas and social order. God is one and 'Alī Muḥammad is the mirror in which He shows Himself and all can see Him. He created the world by the instrumentality of seven attributes, the 'letters of wisdom' which are decree, ordinance, will, resolve, permission, appointed time and book. The Bāb made much of sacred numbers; nineteen is holy. He divided the year into nineteen months of nineteen days each. A college of nineteen members is to rule the community receiving yearly a capital levy of five per cent, unless a man's capital has diminished during the year. It is the duty of the believer to pay this but neither spiritual nor temporal authority can force him to do so. The only punishments allowed are fines and the prohibition of married couples living together for a shorter or longer period. Trade is free and interest on delayed payments is permitted.

Marriage is obligatory at the age of eleven. Divorce is frowned on and there must be a delay of a year to permit of reconciliation. After a month the divorced parties can marry again to a maximum of nineteen times. A widower must marry again after ninety days and a widow after ninety-five under penalty of a fine. Politeness is commanded, silk garments and gold ornaments are allowed. Every year a fast of nineteen days between sunrise and sunset is enjoined on all believers between the ages of eleven and forty-two. Ablutions are recommended though not commanded and every village and town must have its public bath. Women are not veiled and men may talk freely with them though the conversation should not exceed twenty-eight words. The house in which the Bāb was born, that in which he was imprisoned, and the dwellings of his prominent disciples are places of pilgrimage. Travelling by sea is forbidden except to merchants and pilgrims. The only communal prayer is at funerals but sermons are preached in the mosques. For believers there is no ritual impurity; conversion purifies the convert and his property. None may do violence to another. Fermented drinks are prohibited. Once every nineteen days a believer shall invite nineteen guests, even if it is only to a draught of water. Special rules for inheritance were laid down, including a bequest to the deceased's teacher.

Bābī is the name usually given to this sect though they prefer to call themselves Bayānī.

Bahāī (Behāī). After the execution of the Bāb a disciple with the honorific name of Ṣubḥ-i-ezel (dawn of eternity) became the head of the sect. A split soon took place and this man's half-brother Bahā Allāh (glory of God) was followed by the great majority. He claimed to be the man referred to by the Bāb in the cryptic words, "He whom God will publicly confirm". His teaching was meant to change the Bābī faith into a world religion.

The right life consists in not doing wrong to any, in loving one another, in suffering injustice without resentment, in keeping goodness always in mind and in helping to heal the sick. The goal is universal peace to be attained by adopting this religion which has no priests and no ceremonies. Every town should build a meeting-house for a committee of nine which guides the community; the money comes from inheritances which lapse to the treasury, fines and a tax of one nineteenth of capital which has to be paid once. Ascetic practices are forbidden for man is made for joy. Every religion contains some truth for it is one spirit which speaks through all prophets as men can hear them. Resurrection is of the spirit only. It is believed that Bahā Allāh is an incarnation of Christ.

Tāūsī. This Persian sect gets its name from a man who was nicknamed *tāūs* (peacock) from his fondness for fine clothes, something unbecoming in a mystic; the real founder appears to have been a disciple, Ḥājjī Mullā Sulṭān who was head of the sect from 1876 till his death in 1909. They believe that in every age a representative of God with unlimited powers is on earth and his authority extends over all men's activities, confirming or cancelling previous codes of law. He is apostle, imam, *quṭb* and reveals himself in different forms to all men or to individuals. Moses, 'Alī and his descendants, Junaid and his successors, Tāūs and Ḥājjī Mullā Sulṭān were in turn this representative; through him everything is. There has always been occultation and manifestation; each one is the sealer of his predecessors and the opener for his successors. He is the centre of the circle of the vice-gerency of God, the circumference and the unmoved pole, the great sphere of movements too swift to be perceived, and he who causes the spheres to move at different speeds. Because of his angelic nature he is hidden from those who have not attained perfection but by his kingly power visible to the perfected disciples who have attained to seeing the angelic being. One of these persons, who possess these qualities, will cause himself to be seen completely. The mission of each one is Muḥammad's. The representative has an innate and universal knowledge of all men and all things in the world; this can be called innate holiness as opposed to religious holiness which a disciple can attain when he does homage to the representative or his *quṭb* and vows to him complete obedience.

In this system the *quṭb* is above the imam; those outside the sect are not worthy of salvation but most Muslims will join it with their last breath. The process of initiation is in four stages in which the likeness and will of the *quṭb* takes the place of the name of God in the heart of the disciple and he trains himself to gaze into his consciousness and recite the litany at the same time, an extremely hard if not impossible task, except for the space of a few moments.

The ritual shows a likeness to that of the Ahl-i-ḥaqq so this sect is a typical example of a modern heterodox syncretism uniting ideas from the mystics, the Ahl-i-ḥaqq and the Bābī system.

India with its mixed population provides many irritants which stir the Muslim conscience to activity. Many of the converts from Hinduism—especially where mass conversion occurred—brought over into their new faith ideas and practices which were contrary to Islam. Some do not approve of the re-marriage of widows and some Hindu shrines are visited by Muslims for religious purposes. Wahhābī ideas spread to India and were welcomed. Sharī'at Allāh founded the Farāiḍī sect about the year 1804 in Bengal. He confined his activity to the reform of religion and had great influence. He forbade the special Friday and festival prayers because they could only be observed in a land ruled by Muslims; he forbade the handgrip at the initiation of a student and demanded a confession of sin and a declaration of a resolve to live a life well pleasing to God. He roused violent opposition by his ruling that, when a birth took place, the father should cut the umbilical cord and not the midwife.

His son, Dūdhū Miyān was more politically minded; he organized the sect in districts each with its own head, he terrorized the peasants into joining the sect and helped them against the illegal actions of the landlords. He proclaimed that all men are equal, that the earth belongs to God, and that human ownership and rent are wicked. He made himself judge for his followers and punished those of them who resorted to the Government courts. He died in 1860 and the sect is decreasing. On Friday they observe the ordinary midday prayer instead of the special prayer with the sermon.

Sayyid Aḥmad of Bareilly preached a return to a pure and simple worship free from all superstitions and the worship of prophets and apostles. He was saluted as the caliph or as mahdī and forced conversion of Hindus occurred. In 1823 he prepared a holy war to free the Muslims of the Punjab from the oppression of the Sikhs; after several years of fighting he was killed and his army dispersed in 1831. A pupil, Karāmat 'Alī, carried on the religious side of his work, joining the Farāiḍī movement in 1855 though he held that the Friday prayer was incumbent on Indian Muslims in spite of their not being the rulers.

Ahmaḍī. India has provided an unusual manifestation of the mahdī idea. In 1880 Mirzā Ghulām Aḥmad Khān of Qadian in the Punjab published *barāhīn-i-aḥmadiya* (Aḥmadi Proofs) which contains the germs of his teaching though it was not till 1889 that he allowed homage to be done to himself as mahḍī, obtaining a few followers. Two years later he claimed to be both Messiah and mahdī, asserting that his coming was foretold in the Old Testament, the New and the Koran. The verse, "O children of Israel! Of a truth I am God's apostle to you to confirm the law which was given before me, and to announce an apostle to you that shall come after me whose name shall be Aḥmad", referred not to Muḥammad but to Ghulām Aḥmad. He claimed that revelation identified him with Jesus, one of the proofs being his likeness in character to Jesus, but afterwards he claimed to be superior to him. In 1904 he claimed to be a manifestation of Krishna. Son of God, sun of righteousness and manifestation of the Arabian prophet were titles which he applied to himself; he came in the spirit and power of Jesus. Ghulām Aḥmad did not pretend to be a prophet in his own right but only in and through Muḥammad; he received messages from God but not revelation. One of the proofs of his mission was his power to foretell the deaths of his enemies; there was a suspicion that his followers had a hand in the fulfilment of these prophecies so the Government forbade him to exercise this power.

The alleged decadence of Islam was the opportunity for Ghulām Aḥmad because a time of disturbance and moral degradation should precede the coming of the mahdī. He insisted that religion is an affair of the spirit; the mere repetition of the confession and the mechanical performance of religious duties like prayer and pilgrimage are not enough. He would have nothing to do with politics—this is one aspect of his loyalty to the Government. His mahdī was a man of peace, an idea new to Islam; his mission was to spread the truth by preaching not by fighting so this involved a change in the idea of the holy war which was to be conducted by missionaries, not by soldiers. The new sect set itself in opposition to other Muslims; the members were not allowed to pray behind an imam who was not of the sect, to attend the funerals of other Muslims or to give their daughters to them in marriage. In accord with precedent, a man might marry a woman from outside the sect. Mystical practices, the worship of saints and asceticism were banned. In 1900 the Government recognized Aḥmadi as the name of the sect; previously it had been called Qadiani or Mirzaï.

On the death of Ghulām Aḥmad authority was divided between his deputy and a committee but no friction followed because the deputy acted as the servant of the committee. On his death a son of the founder was chosen as leader and, as he showed signs of being an autocrat, a split took place.

Those who followed the new head, emphasized the differences between themselves and other Muslims and tended to make Ghulām Aḥmad a prophet. In December there is a gathering of the faithful at Qadian and it is doubtful whether the founder would approve the respect which is shown to his tomb. A successful school is maintained at Qadian.

The seceders made Lahore their headquarters and aim at minimizing the differences between themselves and other Muslims. The most they will admit is that Ghulām Aḥmad is the latest renewer of religion, one of whom is expected every hundred years. They appeal to all Muslims for funds and carry on active missionary work; they have lately sent missionaries to several countries in Europe. One of their leaders has published in English a translation of the Koran with notes and a thick volume on Islam.

Another small secession maintains itself in the Deccan; Muslim sects have always been fissiparous.

Jamāl al-dīn al-Afghāni (1838/9-1897), one of the most remarkable figures in Islam in the century, was called by his friends a great patriot and by enemies a dangerous agitator. He was a mighty force in the liberal and constitutional movements of the time, working indefatigably for the release of Muslim states from European influence and spoliation, the setting up of liberal government, and the union of all Muslim states including the Shī'a, to resist Europe. Apart from politics, he lives not in his own work but in his pupils of whom Muḥammad 'Abduh was the chief.

Muḥammad 'Abduh (1849?–1905) of Egypt became the leader of those who felt that something was wrong with Islam and yet remained faithful to it. He was convinced that any revival of Islam must be a return to the teaching of Muḥammad, to a true understanding of the Koran. He taught that God can only be known by revelation but what He is is for ever hidden from men for reason cannot penetrate the mystery of His being, as a tradition says, "Reflect upon the creation of God, but do not reflect upon His essence, lest you perish". Within the sphere of religion there is a place for reason. Religion is a general sense, the province of which is to discover means of happiness which are not directly discernible by reason. But it is reason which has the final authority in the recognition of this sense, and in directing the exercise of it in the sphere for which it was given, and in the acceptance of the beliefs and rules of conduct which this sense discovers for it. Belief in the existence of God is a fundamental article of faith, and this belief is founded upon reason, so the priority of reason in Islam is apparent. Reason cannot contradict revelation; the more reason can discover, the more it glorifies God. It is obvious that the thinking is confused. Besides the attributes of God which can be known by reason, there are others which cannot be so known, although they are not contrary to it. These have been made known by revelation; they are speech and hearing.

In his teaching on predestination and free will Muḥammad ʻAbduh is practically a Muʻtazilī; he rebuts the charge, so common in western books, that Islam teaches fatalism, denying that any Muslim of his day, of whatever sect, held the view of complete compulsion or believed that free choice had been taken from him entirely. He does not hold the Muʻtazilī view that God must do the best He can for men, that this is the best of all possible worlds for them; but this world has a perfection of its own because it proceeds from the necessarily existent, Who is perfect. As Muḥammad was the medium through whom God revealed Himself to men, prophecy is at the centre of religion; the discussion follows familiar lines.

One of the objects of religion is to make men happy in this world by ennobling their characters and freeing them from base passions. If they will not accept it, the full consequences may not be visible in the individual for the wicked may be successful as this world counts success; but they are visible in the nation for a people that deserts God is bound to degenerate and perish. Christianity is condemned because it forgets the nature of man by teaching an extravagant tenderness for others, the mortification of the body and detachment from the world.

The Muslims in India were discontented under the English Government for various reasons and one manifestation of their dislike was the boycott of the Government schools which the divines declared to be contrary to Muslim law. One result was that they shut themselves out of Government service. The man who changed this was (Sir) Sayyid Aḥmad Khān. He preached and worked for loyalty to the Government urging that India could not be considered 'an abode of war' because Muslims were free to follow all the dictates of their faith. He was equally convinced that a change in their religious outlook was necessary. He was in essentials orthodox; he had no doubt that Muḥammad was possessed of all the authority which should belong to the last and greatest of the prophets, that the Koran was the final revelation of God, and that sound tradition told the truth about Muḥammad and his work. But he insisted on men's individual right to interpret these in the light of reason for nature and reason uphold the authority which Muḥammad claims for himself. He followed the orthodox view that reason cannot contradict revelation for religion is based on nature and there is one Lord of both nature and revelation. The importance he attached to reason provoked the conservatives for whom religion consisted in being faithful to the ideas and practices of the past.

Strong in his faith that reason cannot harm religion he laboured without ceasing to improve Muslim education and founded the college at Aligarh, now the Muslim university, where Muslim faith and Western learning should walk hand in hand. With education went social reform; he had no hesitation in sitting at meat with Christians, condemned the veiling of women, and insisted on the need for educating them.

The opposite view was expressed in Morocco. "The most important thing was not to adopt the manners of the Franks for these had caused great damage to the Muslims; they wanted to learn the art of war to defend religion, but in this learning they lost religion."

Sir Muhammad Iqbal (†1938) wrote on Persian metaphysics and was a poet in the lineage of the mystics so it is not surprising that he faced the problem set by the twentieth century to Islam. His starting point is the reality of religious experience; the senses provide the raw material for the natural sciences and communion with God is the matter for the student of religion. The physicist, influenced by the subject matter of his studies, inclines to a mechanical view of the universe and sees nothing beyond the machine. Biology does not support the idea of mechanism. Philosophers with their cosmological, teleological and ontological arguments cannot prove that God is. Communion with Him is the only proof that He is. Religious teachers call the organ by which men know God, the heart. It is the essential man, not a mysterious special faculty; it is a mode of dealing with reality in which the external senses play no part. The mystic state is marked, 1. by immediacy; nothing comes between a man and his God; 2. it is a whole which cannot be analysed into component parts; 3. it is a moment of intimate association with a unique other self, transcending and suppressing personality; 4. it cannot be communicated; 5. yet it is a state in some way related to everyday life; the mystic and prophet return to normal levels with an added sense of authority.

For the doctrine of God Iqbal has assimilated the best that modern scientific and philosophical thought can teach him. The Koran likens God to light; this is interpreted to mean not His all-pervasiveness but that He is the absolute, for light is the nearest approach to the absolute. There is no place for a deistic creator. From the standpoint of the all-inclusive ego there is no 'other'. In Him thought and deed, the act of knowing and the act of creating, are identical. This is not pantheism for God is eternally creating. Iqbal quotes with approval a Western writer who says that the universe is a structure of events possessing the character of a continuous creative flow. This view is supported by the Koran which speaks frequently of the succession of night and day. The fundamental concepts of science, space, time and matter are interpretations which thought puts on the free creative energy of God. In this creative stream man holds a peculiar place. He is not the slave of external forces; the emergence of egos endowed with the power of spontaneous action, the results of which therefore cannot be foreseen, is, in a sense, a limitation of the freedom of the all-inclusive ego. But this limitation is not imposed from without; it is born out of His own creative freedom. The ultimate reality is spiritual and its life consists in its temporal activity. When Ḥallāj said, "I am the creative truth", he affirmed the reality and permanence of the human ego in a profounder personality.

In dealing with predestination Iqbal adopts the double idea of real and serial time. Conscious existence is life in time. On its efficient side it enters into relation with what we call the world of space. A deeper analysis of conscious experience reveals the appreciative side of the self. It is only in moments of profound meditation, when the efficient self is in abeyance, that we sink into our deeper self and reach the inner centre of experience. There is change and movement in it but they are wholly non-serial in character. The time of the appreciative self is a single 'now' which the efficient self, in its traffic with the world of space, pulverizes into a series of 'nows'. To prove this he quotes the Koran:

> And put thou thy trust in Him that liveth and dieth not, and celebrate His praise . . . who in six days created the heavens and the earth, and whatever is between them, then mounted the throne: the God of mercy. . . .
>
> All things have We created after a fixed decree; Our command was but one word, swift as the twinkling of an eye.

Pure time is an organic whole in which the past is not left behind, but is moving along with, and operating in the present. Destiny is time regarded as prior to the disclosure of its possibilities; it is time freed from the net of causal sequence; it is the inward reach of a thing, the possibilities lying in the depths of its nature which can be realized and come into being successively without any feeling of external compulsion.

Islam does justice to both worlds, the here and the hereafter. The modern Muslim has to re-think the whole system of Islam without completely breaking with the past; the whole legal and theological system must be overhauled. In the language of the schools the way of *ijtihād* is still open. The great legists never claimed finality for their constructions and none of the four 'principles of law' are immutable. No machinery for fixing 'agreement' was ever set up; 'analogy' can still be applied; Abū Ḥanīfa did without 'tradition' though it has its place as a counterpoise to doctrinaire rationalism; the main purpose of the Koran is to awaken in man a higher consciousness of his relation to God and the universe and critics will find that the rules laid down in it for daily life are wiser than they suspected.

It will be guessed from the last sentence that Iqbal was conservative in any practical suggestions he made for reform because he was convinced of the superiority of Islam. Whether the religion can stand the very new wine he tried to pour into it, only the future can show.

The pressure of Western ideas has made one change in the thought of Islam; in the Middle Ages Muslims ignored other systems of thought but now they have to meet the arguments of outsiders against their faith. They try to show that true humanity, morality and reason find their highest expression in the law and doctrine of Islam. They admit that their religion today is not what it might be, that reform is necessary, but insist that only Islam as it ought to be, can meet the needs of mankind. Circumstances have changed and demand some change in the religious system.

The influence of Ghazālī on Muḥammad 'Abduh was strong; it is shown clearly in the conception of the religious life as something inward and vital, an affair of the heart, to which outward forms are but secondary and contributory. Those, who may be called loosely disciples of Muḥammad 'Abduh, came also under the influence of the later members of the Ḥanbalī school of theology. This had called for the rejection of all innovations and a return to the simplicity of early Islam. It was convenient for the reformers to claim that they were only following the example of the past. Their programme of reform included the following: "to promote social, religious, and economic reforms to prove the suitability of Islam as a religious system under present conditions, and the practicability of the Divine Law as an instrument of Government; to remove superstitions and beliefs that do not belong to Islam, and to counteract false teachings and interpretations of Muslim beliefs, such as prevalent ideas of predestination, the bigotry of the different Schools, or Rites, of Canon law, the abuses connected with the cult of saints and the practices of the Sufi orders; to encourage tolerance and unity among the different sects; to promote general education, together with the reform of text-books and methods of education, and to encourage progress in the sciences and arts; and to arouse the Muslim nations to competition with other nations in all matters which are essential to national progress."

These men worked towards various ends; some were nationalists; some were interested in scholarship and freedom of thought; others insisted on the need for religious reform as the beginning of any improvement. These under Ḥanbalī influence became in some directions more conservative than the conservatives, the spirit of Ghazālī fading out of their lives. They claim to be moderates, mediating between the orthodox, whose strength lies in the blind devotion of the common people, and the ultra-progressive element who favour complete freedom of thought, the adoption of modern civilization, modern forms of Government, and man-made laws. They affirm that Islam, if interpreted according to their principles, will provide the only solution for modern social, political, and religious problems.

During the last century most Muslim countries saw introduced civil and penal codes which were based on European models. It was only in family life that the sacred law continued unchanged, ruling marriage, divorce, inheritance and private *waqfs*. The average man would say that the first three of these are governed by definite rules laid down in the Koran. If the Koran is the word of God, how can these rules be changed? This is the problem before the reformer. The usual solution is to say that the schools of law have built up a system which does not represent the spirit of Islam; therefore the present age must go behind them, back, to the sources of religion, and make a new system. The rulings of the Koran itself are explained away. It says that a man may marry four wives but in accord with its habit it adds a proviso, he must treat them all alike, "if you cannot deal equitably and justly with all, you shall marry only one". This is made the principal clause so, as absolute justice in matters of feeling is impossible, this injunction amounts to a prohibition of polygamy. Similarly with the veil; "to suppose that he (Muḥammad) ever intended his recommendation should assume its present inelastic form, or that he ever allowed or enjoined the seclusion of women, is wholly opposed to the spirit of his reform".

Books by Muslims on the history of their religion have to be read with caution because they read the ideas of their own day into the Koran and *sunna* and make Muslims of the first generation think and act like men of the twentieth century. The ideas of Muḥammad were capable of development but it is absurd to suppose that the Companions saw in them the implications which are seen today. Tabus are explained as anticipations of the laws of hygiene and jinn are interpreted as microbes. The writers argue from first principles and not from the facts. Obsessed by the glories of early Islam they are never tired of saying that no Muslim of that age could have done an unworthy act and, of a later period, that no prominent man could have harboured an heretical thought. History contradicts these ideas. Perhaps unconsciously, they have felt the influence of Christianity and feel a constant urge to prove that Islam is in no way inferior in its doctrines, morals, and social results. It is safe to say that much of what they claim for Islam is not visible in its history, whatever may be true of the present. Their conception of religion is static; they read the present into the past.

The lawyer divines, who represent traditional Islam, are usually ignorant of European languages and so know very little about the ideas which are seeping into the minds of those who have received a Western education, and so cannot meet their needs. Their policy is to resist every change or innovation as long as possible. The civil and penal codes have been accepted though they overrode prescriptions of the Koran, yet a bill to revise the law on marriage and divorce was condemned as irreligious although the changes proposed were modest. In the same way a book on literature was condemned and withdrawn from circulation because it suggested that Abraham had never lived; the Koran talks of him so he must have been a real man. So far Western ideas have not penetrated beyond the educated class so the mass of the people are content to go on as they are, guided by the orthodox divines.

The problems facing the modernist are economic, social and religious; he knows that something ought to be done but he does not know what. Private *waqfs*, a means of evading the law of inheritance, are sanctioned by the law though not expressly by the Koran; they are an obstacle to the economic life of the country but to attack them is to attack the sacred law and consequently religion. The problems of divorce and marriage have already been mentioned.

The abolition of the caliphate by the Turks was a shock to the Muslim world though the office had for centuries existed in name only. It had a sentimental value. Some suggested that a caliph with only spiritual functions should be elected. This would have been an innovation for the caliph had had no spiritual functions, being the servant of the law not its master; his function had been to see that the law was obeyed and how could he do this if he had no force behind him! Such a caliph would be more like the imam of the Shī'a; besides there is no machinery for appointing him and never has been. The nearest approach to such a functionary is the unofficial corporation of divines; these were not appointed but won their position by learning and force of personality; the clearest example of the agreement of the community.

In theory the nationalists, those who held that the salvation of Islam depended on the building up of strong independent Muslim states, were committing the sin of breaking the unity of the community. But in the past separate states have existed without damage to the unity and there is no reason why the same should not happen again. The tradition, "The differences of my people are a blessing to them", may prove true in the political field.

The modernists have not been able or have not tried to question the authority of the Koran as the word of God but accept it as the foundation of religion. They have interpreted it to mean the opposite of what it says, have read into it meanings that would have astonished Muḥammad if he could have understood them but, in so doing, they have followed vaguely liberal ideas and have had no consistent philosophy to guide them. Their method was entirely subjective. Any attempts to form a critical estimate of the Koran have faded away and no one hints that there is in it a human element which has to be judged like other things human. The traditional, mechanical view of revelation is maintained; a body of truth was delivered to the prophets who were merely tools for passing it on to others. The idea that the revelation made to a prophet, in spite of being greater than he, is part of his life, grows out of it and shares its weakness, is not accepted. The psychological study of prophecy has not begun.

Influenced probably by the Christian reverence for Jesus, Muslims have elevated Muḥammad to the position of the ideal man and have made religion to be the imitation of him. The attitude to him has varied during the centuries.

He himself stated that his function was to be a messenger of God to man; he was a man among other men and had no power to work signs and miracles. Christians arguing with Muslims laid stress on the miracles recorded in the Bible as evidences of its truth; so much so that it has been said that they forced the Muslims to turn Muḥammad into a miracle worker. Orthodox Islam now believes that prophets work miracles. Popular Islam goes much further in its reverence for Muḥammad; he committed no sins, even before his call. Supernatural gifts were attributed to him, "He could see in front, also behind and in the dark; did he walk with one who was taller than he, he equalled him in height; sitting down his shoulders were above those who sat with him; his body threw no shadow because he was all light". He was the model of manly beauty, the highest morality consists in imitating him; many of the ideas connected with the 'light' of Muḥammad have become the common property of Muslims. When he went to heaven on the night journey, he started to take off his shoes before entering heaven but God told him to keep them on, for heaven would be honoured by the touch of them. Wahhābīs reject this extreme veneration for Muḥammad. The modernists avoid the crasser forms of adulation but make him the centre and pivot without whom there can be no religion. They ignore whatever does not fit in with this conception. In the same way they read history, choosing the nobler persons and incidents and turning a blind eye to the darker sides, thus proving to their own satisfaction that Islam is the noblest work of God.

The gulf between the lawyer-divine and the mystic remains. The divine reverences a transcendent God who is separate from the world and is not touched by a feeling for man's infirmities; the mystic seeks rest in a God who is ever present with him. The God of theology is impassible; remote from all human feeling he hands out to men good fortune or ill, eternal bliss or eternal misery, indifferent to the gratitude of the one and the plaints of the other. The sole reason why men should act rightly is that God has so ordained; blind obedience to an irrational command is the highest they can aim at. In the presence of God man is a slave and even that is too dignified a name to describe adequately his abjectness. Love to God can only be shown by obedience to Him. The God of the mystic is close to him, even in him, is the object of a fervent passion that obliterates the gap between them and allows man to lose himself in the deity and to become one with Him.

So long as the antagonism between these two conceptions endures, the task of re-thinking Islam, which Iqbal demanded, will remain undone. Both sides may find encouragement in the Koran which declares that 'nothing is like God' and also asserts that He is 'nearer to man than the vein in his neck'.

CHAPTER XI

CONCLUSION

MUḤAMMAD is often called Muṣṭafā (Chosen) so a man feels that in following him he becomes one of a chosen people and looks down on all others. Hence the exclusiveness of Muslim literature; the words put into the mouth of the second caliph about the books in the library of Alexandria, "If they agree with the Koran, they are unnecessary; if they contradict it, they are wrong" exemplify this frame of mind. At the other end of the scale is the tribesman of South Arabia of whom it is said, "Nor does architectural splendour or artistic beauty impress him except to earn a bitter curse, and the sneering comment *kufr* (idolatry), accompanied by symbolic expectoration". This temper has passed in some quarters but only among the minority. It is tempting to suggest that the sterility which befell Islam was the result of spiritual inbreeding; too proud to notice anything outside the pale, it missed the stimulus of fresh ideas and failed to bring anything new out of its own store. Take as an example the polemic against Christianity; it is hardly too much to say that, till quite recently, the latest book on the subject was only a re-hash of the earliest. In such circumstances it was possible to say that the main object of the study of the Koran was the deduction of rules of conduct from it. In spite of the sterility, during the eighteenth and nineteenth centuries Islam continued to expand, carried outwards by its unofficial missionaries.

The conviction that God is, and is the ruler of the world, gives confidence and dignity to life; it gives "that backbone of character, that firmness of determination and strength of will, and also that uncomplaining patience and submission in the presence of the bitterest misfortune, which characterize and adorn the best adherents of the creed". The Muslim is sure that his faith will give him bliss in this world and the next. A traveller describes an outbreak of cholera. "Cholera dogged our trail. . . . It struck in bivouac after bivouac, and sometimes on the march itself. . . . Though the combatant contingent grew morose, and watched each other with haunted eyes for the first fell signs of the Smiter, there was no panic among them. Islam may be materialistic, and observed with no more consistency than other creeds, while the acts and thoughts of its less civilized adherents often merit the common epithet 'ignorant fanaticism'; but religion is a reality to them, not to be assumed with Levitical attire, but part of their daily life. Hence, in time of stress, it stands them in good stead, and, as officers of Mohammedan corps know well, in the day of red peril, is seldom invoked in vain. It has no less effect, though not so strikingly manifest, when the Slayer stalks abroad in black."

Organized missionary activity has begun. A few years ago the most important society in India was the Anjuman Hidāyat al-Islām in Delhi to which twenty-four other societies in different parts of the country were affiliated. The Lahore branch of the Aḥmadī movement sends missionaries to several countries in Europe. Still, the best proof that Islam is alive lies in its unofficial activities. The strongest bond between Muslims is the pilgrimage which brings together believers from all parts of the world to pray in that place to which they daily turn their faces. No better means could have been imagined for impressing on the minds of the faithful a sense of their common life and of their brotherhood in the faith. At the same time throughout the world the hearts of believers are lifted up in sympathy with their more fortunate brethren gathered in the sacred city, as in their own homes they celebrate the festival of sacrifice. The visit to Mecca has been to many Muslims the experience that has stirred them up to 'strive in the path of God' and become emissaries of their faith. The five daily prayers are an effective means of winning and retaining converts.

Islam has not forgotten the charity to the poor inculcated by Muḥammad and, though its practice may shock the theorists of the west, it is in accord with the temper of the people. An orphan boy heard that he could get education at Aligarh so he made his way thither and was not turned away. Respect for learning is real and the career of the scholar is open to all even if the field of knowledge is narrow. On the whole Islam has been tolerant of other faiths though a conqueror has combined his conquests with the slaughter of idolaters to the greater glory of God. In the Middle Ages the Jews were better off in Muslim than in Christian lands. At times Christians were persecuted, it might be better to say that they suffered from riots and tumults but these were usually provoked by the arrogance and greed of the victims. Examples have been given of Muslim divines standing up for the rights of *dhimmīs*. There seems to be no doubt that the massacres of Armenians in Turkey were engineered by the Government. Usually authority restrained the violence of the mob. Often the motive for attacks on other religions has been dislike of the foreigner rather than religious hatred. In North Africa folk go to the dervish orders for spiritual council rather than to the officials of the mosque for these are paid by the Government and so suspect.

Muḥammad might forbid the killing of bees and ants, Mu'tazilī theologians argue that animals went to heaven as a recompense for their sufferings on earth and that reason could not prove that the killing of them for food was right, the bedouin might pamper his horse (if he had not exchanged it for a motor), but the lot of domestic animals is hard. Religion is not the cause of cruelty but it might have done more to stop it. By gathering the scum from sensational newspapers it would be possible to draw a lurid picture of morals, or lack of them, in Muslim lands but it would be unjust. Muslims tell you that few men have more than one wife; missionaries contradict this. Perhaps the two sets of informants know different social groups. A refined moral sense is shown in a Turkish catechism which condemns, among other sins, envy (though it is permitted to wish that a rich man who uses his wealth in evil ways may lose it), fear of poverty, toadying the rich, despising the poor and hasty judgement on believers. Even the Muslim's pride peeps out; it does not matter what he thinks of other faiths.

In conclusion a quotation from a Ḥanbalī divine shows that even in that arid soil the spirit of religion could flourish.

> "When God illumines the soul, man sees why he was created, that the world passes away, does not keep its promises

to its sons, kills its lovers, and that he must spend the rest of his worthless life trying to make good his sins of omission, and seizing that opportunity the loss of which means the loss of all good. He sees that he cannot count God's mercies to him and, if He called him to account for one of them, He would demand all his labours, so that his only hope of salvation is in the pardon and goodness of God. He sees that if he could do all the righteous acts of men and jinn, they would be as nothing compared to the greatness of God, even if they were his own; but they are the acts of God who made them easy for him and helped him to do them. He sees that God will not accept what man thinks is his own; that what is man's own is only evil, while his good deeds are God's charity to him, which is entirely undeserved. Herein is the foundation of all righteousness! He sees the defects of his own character and his failures to do his duty; and this knowledge, joined to his knowledge of the divine blessings, forbids him to hold up his head so that he comes humbly to God, begging for forgiveness."

GLOSSARY

ADHĀN. Among *sunnī* Muslims the call to prayer consists of seven phrases:

1. God is very great.
2. I testify that there is no god but God.
3. I testify that Muḥammad is the messenger of God.
4. Come to prayer.
5. Come to salvation.
6. God is very great.
7. There is no god but God.

Phrases 2 to 6 are said twice, 7 once, and 1 four times (by the Mālikī school twice). There are some other refinements. A man praying alone or with his family repeats the call aloud. There is no fixed melody; "in Mecca different tunes can often be heard at the same time." Some of the Ḥanbalī rite condemn the singing of the call. The interval between the call and the prayer varies; the call is repeated in the mosque immediately before the service and is called the 'constitution'. For festivals and eclipses the call is, "Come to the congregational prayer".

'ĀRIF. Active participle of the verb 'to know', one who has direct, intuitive knowledge of God; translated by gnostic. The abstract noun is *ma'rifa*. Book-learning is *'ilm*.

ĀYA. Sign and then 'verse' of the Koran.

THE BLACK STONE (*al-ḥajar al-aswad*). The stories about this contradict each other. Adam built the Ka'ba after a model sent down from heaven and sat on the black stone. The Ka'ba was destroyed by the flood and the black stone was hidden in Abū Qubais, a mountain overlooking Mecca. The Ka'ba was not destroyed in the flood. Abraham with the help of Ishmael built the Ka'ba and Gabriel brought the black stone from heaven; it was then white but turned black through its contact with the impurity and sin of the heathen.

BOOK. The people of the book (*ahl al-kitāb*) are those to whom a sacred book has been revealed by God; the Koran names the Jews, Christians and Ṣābians. Nobody knows what this last name means. When the pagans of Harran, the last adherents of the Hellenistic religion, were summoned to embrace Islam on pain of death; some were converted but some saved themselves by claiming to be Ṣābians and so under the protection of God and His apostle. No one could contradict them. After much debate the Zoroastrians were admitted to be people of the book and received the same privileges. People of the book might be called a religious name; in law they are commonly called *dhimmī*.

CALIPH. From the Arabic *khalīfa*, deputy, successor. The ruler, who calls himself caliph, claims to be the successor of Muḥammad in his political capacity. Adam, the first prophet, is called the *khalīfa* of God on earth. The later caliphs were also called *khalīfa* of God which has been explained to mean legitimate caliph.

CONVENT. Several words are thus translated. *Ribāṭ* was originally a fortified post on the frontier or sea coast to protect Muslim territory or serve as a base for raids into foreign lands. The root means 'tie up' and the word denotes the place where the horses and other animals were kept. These posts were often garrisoned by volunteers who devoted the intervals between fighting to pious exercises under the guidance of a pious scholar in preparation for a martyr's death. Later the word came to mean any house where men of religion dwelt together. There were also *ribāṭs* for women. *Rābiṭa* is a hermitage to which a holy man withdrew and where he lived with his disciples.
Zāwiya (corner) denoted first a small mosque or prayer-room. In the west it may denote a hermitage. It has come to mean the convent of a dervish order and so equal to *ribāṭ*. This usually contains a mosque, a room for the recitation of the Koran, a Koran school, and rooms for the residents, guests and travellers. The mother-house of an order will also have the founder's tomb surmounted by a dome. There may be a cemetery for those who wish to be buried near the holy man. In Turkish

tekke is the ordinary name for a convent and *khānqah* is a Persian loan word; it seems not to have been restricted to *ṣūfī* and dervish establishments.

DĀBBAT AL-ARḌ. The beast of the earth. It will appear in the last days and put a black mark on the faces of unbelievers and a white on the faces of believers; these marks will spread till faces become wholly black or white. It will have the seal of Solomon and Moses' staff and with it he will write 'believer' or 'unbeliever' on the faces of men.

DERVISH. Originally a Persian word meaning poor; it was borrowed into Arabic as *darwīsh* or represented by its equivalent *faqīr*. The phrase, 'he put on the dress of the poor' means that he joined a dervish order.

FĀTIḤA. The first chapter of the Koran; the repetition of it is the commonest act of worship.

Praise be to God, Lord of the worlds!
The compassionate, the merciful!
King on the day of reckoning!
Thee *only* do we worship, and to Thee do we cry for help.
Guide Thou us on the straight path,
The path of those to whom Thou hast been gracious; with whom Thou art not angry, and who go not astray.

FIṬRA. An infinitive meaning 'manner of creation'. A tradition runs, "Every child is born in the *fiṭra*, its parents make of it a Jew, Christian or Magian". The obvious sense is that every child is born a Muslim and stays so till it reaches the age of discretion. This is the Mu'tazilī explanation but it raises legal and theological problems; e.g. if a child is a Muslim it cannot inherit from parents of another faith. The assumption underlying the tradition is that Islam is the natural religion of all though many are perverted.

GRAVE. The corpse must be able to sit up to answer the questions of the angels Munkar and Nakīr. There are two ways of contriving this; either a narrow trench is sunk at the bottom of the grave and covered with flagstones or a niche is made at the side and a wall of bricks built to keep out the earth. There is no preference for either form. Both are said to be pre-Islamic. When Muḥammad died, they sent for grave-diggers and the first-comer was employed to dig the type to which he was accustomed. The niche is called *laḥd* and from this root comes the name for heretic *mulḥid*, he who turns aside from the straight path.

ḤARĀM and ḤALĀL. These words go back to an early stage of religion before it had become moral when *harām* was equal to *tabu* and *ḥalāl* meant the opposite of this. A thing might be *ḥarām* because it was connected with the divine or because it was opposed to it. At that stage of thought holiness was infectious and any clash of the holy with the unholy was fraught with danger. The same idea underlies the Jewish question, "does a certain book defile the hands?" meaning, is it part of the canon of scripture? The Old Testament is holy, when touched, some of that holiness comes off on the hands so, before returning to the business of everyday life, the reader must remove that dangerous holiness. In a like manner the Arabs made the circuit of the Ka'ba naked; if their clothes came in contact with the sacred place, they were impregnated with holiness and so useless for ordinary affairs. Later pilgrims borrowed clothes from the inhabitants of Mecca; they were continually in touch with the divine so a little holiness did not matter. The sentence, "they shed *ḥarām* blood in the *ḥarām* place" exhibits two senses of the word so it must be rendered, "they shed blood, which they had no right to shed, in the holy place". Mecca with its environs is a *ḥaram*, sacred, so hunting is forbidden there; pig is unclean and *ḥarām* but wine, though *ḥarām*, is not unclean. Nowadays *ḥalāl* means lawful and *ḥarām*, usually, unlawful. Ḥarīm and iḥrām both denote the special dress worn by pilgrims; they have entered into a close relation with the divine.

HERETICS. Those who deviate only a little from orthodoxy are called *ahl al-ahwā*, people of desires, those who follow the devices and desires of their own hearts or *ahl al-bid'a*, people of innovation or *mulhid*, one who turns aside. Extremists of any sort, especially of the Shī'a or the Khārijīs are called *ghulāt* (plural of *ghālī*) from a verb meaning to boil, be expensive.

ḤIJĀB. Screen or barrier but nowadays used for amulet. These are very common and take many forms. Passages from the Koran, magic squares or cabalistic signs enclosed in a metal or leather case are employed; the so-called hand of Fāṭima is very common, being painted on houses. Amulets are hung round the necks of animals. A Turk gave to an Englishwoman his greatest treasure, the blue bead, which his mother had sewn on to his first shirt and which had always been on some garment of his till he was over six feet tall.

HIJRA. This is the name given to the exodus of the Muslims from Mecca to Medina, more especially to the flight of Muḥammad. The precise date is not certain but the popular opinion is that he reached Medina on 8 Rabī' I corresponding to 20th September, 622, though the 2nd and 12th are also mentioned. When the Muslims decided to have an era of their own, they fixed on the year of the emigration as the first year. The year of Muhammad's birth was suggested but rejected as too uncertain. The beginning of the era was 1 Muḥarram of the year of the flight and this was 16th July, 622. This decision was taken probably in the year 17. The common transcription in English is Hegira.

IJTIHĀD. The meaning is 'exertion' and in its technical sense the word denotes the trying to solve problems from first principles instead of repeating the solutions of others which is *taqlīd*. *Ijtihād* is possible in the fundamental and secondary problems of law and in philosophy; but commonly the use is restricted to law. It is agreed by all that there can be no difference of opinion on the fundamentals. The Shī'a says that as long as the imam is concealed, his agents, the scholars, can by their 'supreme effort and endeavour' arrive at a complete knowledge of the Koran and traditions. These men are called *mujtahids*; by their learning and personality they gain the respect of the people and exert powerful religious, and consequently political, influence. Some of the followers of Ash'arī and the Mu'tazilīs say that the *mujtahid* cannot make a mistake; the majority say that he is sometimes right and sometimes wrong. If he is wrong, he is rewarded by God for his endeavour and if he is right, he gets double the reward; indeed Muḥammad said, "If you are right, you get ten good things and if you are wrong, one". It is quite certain that, if a *mujtahid* makes a mistake, he has not committed a sin. It has been said that every *mujtahid* is right in his solution of minor problems but it is wrong to say that all are right in the fundamentals of theology for that would lead to affirming that Christians, Zoroastrians and unbelievers are right when they are manifestly wrong.

It is agreed by all except a few modernists that the days of *ijtihād* are over; no one can start again from the beginnings and build up a new school of law; all that is possible is to develop further deductions made by earlier authorities of the four schools. During the ninth and tenth centuries other schools existed but they have died out, probably for political reasons or possibly geographical because wandering scholars in search of a teacher generally kept to beaten tracks, the roads which led the pilgrims to Mecca.

ISHRĀQI. An adjective formed from *ishrāq*, an infinitive meaning the rising of the sun and then illumination. *Mashraqī* means eastern; then it is used as equivalent to *ishrāqī* in its philosophical sense.

KA'BA. The corners of the building point roughly to the four cardinal points. The black stone is built into the east corner breast high from the ground. The door, which can only be reached by a movable flight of steps, for it is six feet above ground level, is on the north-east side near the black stone and the space between the two is *al-multazam*, so-called because worshippers press themselves against that bit of the wall while praying and offering petitions. In the north-west wall is the spout (*mīzāb*) through which water flows off the roof; hanging from the end of it is a board called the 'beard of the spout'. Also on the north-west side is a semi-circular wall (*al-ḥaṭīm*) the ends of which are about six feet from the Ka'ba; the space thus enclosed is *al-ḥijr* and in it Ishmael and his mother are buried. The *ṭawāf* passes outside it. The Ka'ba has been rebuilt several times and once it was enlarged to include *al-ḥijr*. The Ka'ba is covered with the *kiswa*, a dark brocade made in Egypt. There is a band of decorative lettering round the whole cover and the door has a separate curtain with inscriptions embroidered in gold. The old cover is removed a few days before the pilgrimage and replaced by a white cover, 'it puts on its pilgrim dress'; the new cover is put on when the pilgrimage is finished. In the past States have quarrelled over the privilege of providing the cover. The one room in the Ka'ba is practically empty; a ladder in it leads to the roof. This room is ceremonially swept by the most important men present just before the pilgrimage.

KHUṬBA. Sermon, address. During the lifetime of Muḥammad and for some years after public worship was not strictly regulated. The community's meeting for prayer was a convenient opportunity for the ruler to make known his wishes; it appears that the call to prayer was given for this purpose. The address might deal with any matter of public interest; the caliph might be the speaker in the capital. Later this duty was left to an underling. The sermon included a prayer for the sovereign who was mentioned by name; the omission of the name was equivalent to raising the standard of revolt. Later still, the sermon was left to the officials of the mosque and consisted usually of religious and moral platitudes. It is really two sermons separated by a prayer. The preacher (*khaṭīb*) stands for the sermons holding in his hand a staff or a wooden sword (in olden times it might be a bow) and sits for the prayer. This ritual appears to have been borrowed from the practice of the pagan judge or arbitrator.

KORAN. The Arabic is *qur'ān* from a verb 'read, repeat aloud'; in the Koran itself this word is often used for a single revelation.

KUFR. Unbelief; then anything which results from it. As the same root means to be ungrateful, the Khārijīs distinguished between *kufr shirk* or *kufr milla* downright unbelief and *kufr ni'ma* ingratitude for favours, practical unbelief which had not expressed itself as a philosophy. *Kāfir* unbeliever, infidel. Gratitude for favours *shukr ni'ma* also occurs.

LAW. *Sharī'a* is the law as established by God, the whole body of legislation covering worship, personal and social life, business and criminal law. The original meaning of the word is 'path', more especially 'path to water'. The infinitive used adverbially means in a book of law 'legally', in a book of theology 'by revelation'; a clear indication that life cannot be divided into watertight compartments. As something to be studied and developed by men law is *fiqh* and the lawyer is *faqīh*. In the Koran the verb means 'understand'; perhaps *faqīh* is a translation of *jurisprudens*. A way of thinking, body of doctrine is called *madhhab* (way, going) so each legal school or rite is a *madhhab*. The interpretation of the Koran and the studies connected with tradition are held to be, to some extent, part of *fiqh*. The law is concerned with external acts only and takes no account of intentions. No satisfactory classification of laws has been discovered. The usual division is into laws dealing with worship, civil laws and penalties but no importance attaches to it. The Shī'a divides them into those dealing with worship, contracts, one-sided transactions (e.g. gifts), and all those not included under the first three heads.

A popular handbook of the Mālikī school, the *Risāla* of Ibn Abī Zaid of Kairawan, contains 45 chapters. Chapter 1 is theological; 2 to 24 Religious duties; 25 to 27 Legal alms (religious tax) and alms at the breaking of the fast; 28 Pilgrimages; 29 Sacrifices, hunting, circumcision, forbidden food and drink; 30 Holy war; 31 Oaths and vows; 32 to 33 Marriage, divorce, widows, alimony; 34 Sales and similar contracts; 35 Wills, manumission of slaves; 36 Pre-emption, gifts, *waqfs*, pledges, loans, illegal acquisition; 37 Murder, manslaughter, wounds, penalties laid down in the Koran; 38 Judicial decisions, witnesses; 39 Inheritance; 40 Divers religious duties, obligations and commendable practices; 41 Care of the person, circumcision, shaving the head, clothing, etc.; 42 Food and drink; 43 Social rules, recitation of the Koran, petitions to God;

44 Medical care, charms, castration, branding, dogs, kindness to slaves; 45 Dreams, yawning, sneezing, games, racing, archery.

MAḤMAL. Pilgrims travelled to Mecca in companies as on other journeys. Egypt and Syria and sometimes other countries sent an official caravan with a commander, *amīr al-ḥajj*, and a guard This was accompanied since some date in the thirteenth century by a *maḥmal*, a conventionalized litter covered with rich stuffs. (During the journey the cover was packed up.) This litter was a symbol of sovereignty; it was carried on a camel which was led and not ridden. The idea that the *maḥmal* contained the cover for the Ka'ba is quite wrong.

MALĀÏKA. Angels; it is used as the plural of *malak*. The ideas are largely borrowed from the Jews. Several archangels have names. Isrāfīl (probably derived from seraphim) is colossal; his feet are below the seventh earth and his head reaches to the pillars of the throne of God. He initiated Muḥammad into his mission as prophet; then Gabriel took over and began to communicate the Koran to him. Isrāfīl will sound the trump which calls the dead from their graves. Another story says that he will be the first to rise at the resurrection and then will blow the trump. 'Izrāīl is the angel of death; he has two forms, one beautiful in which he approaches a good man, and one hideous in which he draws near to a bad man. When God created death, He called the angels to look at it, but they fell senseless and lay in a swoon for one thousand years. But 'Izrāīl is the lord of death. When God wanted a handful of clay to make Adam, the earth refused it and 'Izrāīl was the only angel strong enough to take it. He draws the soul of a good man gently from his body but tears out an evil soul violently. Michael (Mīkāl, Mikāīl) with Gabriel (Jibrīl) was the first to do obeisance to Adam. God told these two that one of them must die and as neither was ready to sacrifice himself for the other, God said, "Follow the example of 'Alī who was ready to give his life for Muḥammad". Mālik is the guardian of hell, assisted by the Zabāniya. The souls of the spheres are identified with angels.

MASJID. Place of prostration, of worship, mosque. Another name, *jāmi'* was originally reserved for a mosque in which the

Friday prayer was said; in Egypt it has become the ordinary name for any mosque. The mosque has to allow men to stand in rows so the usual type is a rectangle part of which is roofed to protect worshippers from the weather; the open court is often surrounded by colonnades. The simplest form is one room. Lavatories are provided in the bigger ones for the necessary ablutions. Minarets were not built till some fifty years after the death of Muḥammad; the towers of churches or watch towers suggest themselves as models. A mosque need not have one, Wahhābī mosques do not. A dome usually shows that the mosque is also a tomb. A big mosque has a high pulpit beside the niche (*miḥrāb*) where the preacher sits under a canopy. Often there is a platform supported on pillars which is the place of the muezzins during the prayer. Often a section was railed in with a private entrance for the caliph or governor. There is always a clock in the big mosques. Sometimes the public treasury was in the court of the chief mosque of the town. At Hama one of the big water wheels, which are the sights of the town, supplies the mosque with water.

MIRACLE. One worked by a prophet is *mu'jiza* 'that which makes weak', i.e. he who tries to repeat it finds himself unable to do so. Such an act is always accompanied by a challenge to unbelievers. One worked by a saint does not include this challenge; it is called *karāma* 'honour'. In both cases it is God who acts not the man.

MI'RĀJ. The word means ladder and is used to denote Muḥammad's ascent to heaven. The words of the Koran, "Praise to Him who caused His servant to travel by night from the sacred mosque to the furthest mosque" are the starting point of the story. Two journeys are combined, one to Jerusalem and one to heaven; Muḥammad was taken from Mecca to Jerusalem and thence to heaven. The ascent to heaven is also put at the beginning of his mission after an angel or two angels had taken his heart out of his body and cleansed it, the ascent starting from Mecca. Some hold that both the journey and the ascent were visions.

NĀFILA (pl. nawāfil). Works of supererogation; the word is general but is especially used of extra prayers. They must be of the class of 'approved' acts and are an atonement for venial sins.

NĀQŪS. A long plate of wood or metal beaten with a hammer which takes the place of a bell in some eastern churches.

PUNISHMENT. This may be decreed by God or calculated by man.

ḤADD. A penalty fixed by the law and unalterable. There are several. 1. stoning or flogging for sexual offences; 2. flogging for having accused a married woman of adultery; 3. flogging for drunkenness; 4. cutting off the hand for theft; 5. graduated punishments, impalement, mutilation etc., for brigandage. The penalty for drunkenness is in an anomalous position for Muḥammad fixed the penalty at forty stripes wherein Shāfi'ī followed him but the second caliph increased the penalty to eighty stripes and is followed by the three other schools.

TA'ZĪR. A punishment inflicted by the judge according to his estimate of the gravity of the offence. It may be imprisonment, banishment, flogging, or being paraded on a camel or ass with the face blackened. Qiṣāṣ. The *talio*.

QAḌĀ AND QADAR. *Qadar* means arrangement, measure, power; *qaḍā* means to finish, settle, judge. *Qadar* is used both of God's power and man's; used absolutely it refers to God, "His providence whether it brings good fortune or misfortune", to use a stock phrase. The terms are defined thus: *qaḍā* denotes the foreknowledge and eternal will of God which is connected with events in the sum of their surroundings. *Qadar* denotes the coming into being in time of these events with their causes as determined by *qaḍā*. Acts that result from necessary causes are due to this irrevocable decree; voluntary acts of men are known beforehand by God but He knows them as the result of their choice; the occurrence of these acts is not due to His foreknowledge and decree.

RAK'A. A section of the ritual. There are many variations in detail. Standing the worshipper states his intention of performing prayer, recites, 'God is very great', a petition or some apotropaic phrase. Then begins the section. He recites the first chapter of the Koran; some other passage is recited by the imam. The worshipper bends forward till his hands are level with his knees, stands upright and says, 'God hears him who praises Him'. Prostration follows, kneeling and putting the forehead on the ground. He then squats and next makes a second prostration. That ends the section. At certain points in the section the words 'God is very great' and '(I extol) the perfection of my Lord, the great (the most high)' are said. After the prescribed number of sections the confession is said, also blessings on the prophet and the salutation, 'Peace and the mercy of God be on you'. The salutation is said twice. Some say that it is addressed to the guardian angels.

SHAIKH. Old man, elder, chief, teacher. On the mystic path it denotes the adept (synonyms *murshid* [Arabic] and *pīr* [Persian]) who guides the novice (*murīd*) on the way. In the dervish brotherhoods the *shaikh* was usually the head of the order though sometimes this title was reserved to the founder in which case the head was called *khalīfa* (deputy, substitute); the word is anglicized as caliph. Normally the *khalīfa* was personal assistant to the chief. The head of a branch convent was a *muqaddam*. The ordinary member was *akh* (brother, pl. *ikhwān*) or *khādim* (servant). The trade guilds had their chiefs and admission to them was very like admission to an order.

SHIRK. Association, the giving of partners to God; so polytheism or idolatry. *Mushrik* polytheist or idolater.

SIDR. A species of tree, *rhamnus spina Christi*; the noun of unity is *sidra*. The *sidra* of the limit is a tree in paradise near which Muḥammad saw Gabriel.

ṢŪFI. In the east dress is more than a protection against weather, it is often a badge of religion; one, who wore wool, was told to put off his Christianity for wool was the dress of monks. It became the mark of an ascetic. Ṣūfī occurs as part of names in the second half of the eighth century and early in the ninth, there were ṣūfīs in Alexandria who "commanded what was right and forbade what was wrong", men who took religion seriously and used weapons to defend their opinions. Later ṣūfī was restricted to those who practised communion with God. The abstract noun is *taṣawwuf*.

SŪRA. A chapter of the Koran. The word seems to have meant originally a course of stones or bricks.

TAFSĪR. Explanation; in a technical sense the interpretation of the Koran from the points of view of grammar, lexicography, history and theology. Then it denotes a commentary.

TAQLĪD. Imitation. In law it is the opposite of *ijtihād*; the *muqallid* accepts the authority of a teacher and deduces consequences from his rulings. In theology it is the acceptance of beliefs without being able to give reasons for them.

ṬAWĀF. The technical name for a ritual procession round a sanctuary, especially the Ka'ba. At Mecca the circuit has to be made seven times, the first three at the double and the rest walking. The circuit starts at the black stone and the direction is anti-clockwise. The worshipper should kiss or touch the stone each time he passes it but if this is impossible because of the crowd, it is sufficient to halt opposite it. Circumambulation is not peculiar to Mecca. At a celebration near Aden visitors rode or galloped round the holy place, seemingly each man beginning when he chose and stopping when he liked.

TA'WĪL. Allegorical interpretation, especially of the Koran by the mystics.

WALĪ. Protector, benefactor, friend. In current use it denotes a saint, a friend of God, one who enjoys His favour and so possesses superhuman powers; then, as a dead saint still has this power, the word comes to mean a saint's tomb. In law the *walī* is the legal representative of some one. A woman cannot appear at the legal part of the marriage ceremony so she is represented by her *walī*, usually her father. When a man has been killed, his *walī* is the relative on whom lies the duty of blood revenge or of deciding whether to accept blood money.

ZINDĪQ. The word was borrowed in Iraq from the language of the Sasanian administration in which it denoted: 1. a heretic who devised a new, allegorical interpretation of the Avesta and 2. a Manichee. In Arabic it denotes a Manichee, any dualist, a Buddhist monk and later, any free-thinker. It came to mean one whose teaching endangered the State by attacking the honour of the prophet. An inquisition to deal with such people was set up in 783. To be accused as a *zindīq* was more serious than a charge of unbelief.

ZIYĀRA. It means 'visit' generally; then visit (pilgrimage) to the tomb of a saint or any other holy place, especially the tomb of Muḥammad in Medina after performing the pilgrimage to Mecca; then it denotes the holy place itself.

BIBLIOGRAPHY

GENERAL

Encyclopaedia of Islam. Leyden and London. 1913 onwards.
Arnold and Guillaume. *Legacy of Islam.* Oxford. 1931.
I. Goldziher. *Vorlesungen ueber den Islam.* 2nd ed. Heidelberg. 1925.
I. Goldziher (French version) *Le Dogme et la Loi.* Paris. 1920.
Muḥammad ʻAli. *Religion of Islam.* Lahore. 1936.
R. Levy. *Sociology of Islam.* London. Vol. I, 1931. Vol. 2, 1933.
T. W. Arnold. *Preaching of Islam.* 2nd ed. London. 1935.
L. E. Browne. *Eclipse of Christianity in Asia.* Cambridge. 1933.

Translation of the Koran:
Sale; valuable introductory essay. Many editions.
Rodwell. *Everyman* and other editions.
Palmer. Oxford, *World's Classics.*
R. Bell. Edinburgh. Vol. I, 1937. Vol. II, 1939.
H. U. W. Stanton. *The Teaching of the Qur'ān.* London and New York. 1919.

Muḥammad:
Tor Andrae. *Mohammed the Man and his Faith.* London. 1936.
W. Muir. *Life of Mohammed.* Revised edition. Edinburgh. 1923.
W. St. C. Tinsdall. *Sources of the Qur'ān.* London. 1905.

Tradition:
Goldziher. *Mohammedanische Studien*; especially vol. II. Halle; Vol. I, 1888. Vol. II, 1890.
A. Guillaume. *Traditions of Islam.* Oxford. 1924.
D. S. Margoliouth. *Early Development of Mohammedanism.* London. 1914.

Theology:

D. B. MacDonald. *Muslim Theology*. London, 1903.

J. W. Sweetman. *Islam and Christian Theology*. London and Redhill. Vol. I, 1945. Vol. II, 1947.

A. S. Tritton. *Muslim Theology*. London. 1947.

Law:

S. G. Vesey Fitzgerald. *Muhammadan Law*. London. 1931.

Mysticism:

R. A. Nicholson, *Mystics of Islam*. London. 1914.

R. A. Nicholson. *Studies in Islamic Mysticism*. Cambridge. 1921.

Margaret Smith, *Rābi'a the Mystic*. Cambridge, 1928.

Margaret Smith. *Early Mysticism in the Near and Middle East*. London. 1931.

Modern:

D. B. MacDonald. *Religious Attitude and Life in Islam*. Chicago. 1912.

E. W. Lane. *Modern Egyptians*. Many editions.

A. Kennett. *Bedouin Justice*. Cambridge. 1925.

C. C. Adams. *Islam and Modernism in Egypt*. Oxford. 1933.

H. A. R. Gibb. *Modern Trends in Islam*. Chicago. 1947.

M. Titus. *Indian Islam*. Oxford. 1930.

Taha Husain. *An Egyptian Childhood* (trans. E. H. Paxton), London. 1932.

The Muslim Year

The year is lunar containing twelve months and 354 days. The months are:

Muḥarram	Rajab
Ṣafar	Sha'bān
Rabī' I	Ramaḍān
Rabi' II	Shawwāl
Jumādā I	Dhu'l-Qa'da
Jumādā II	Dhu'l-Ḥijja

A rough correspondence with the Christian era can be obtained by the formula (neglecting fractions)

$$\text{A.H.} - \frac{3\ \text{A.H.}}{100} + 621 = \text{A.D.}$$

INDEX

ISLAM

A Books for Libraries Collection

Guillaume, Alfred. **The Traditions of Islam.** 1924

Izutsu, Toshihiko. **The Concept of Belief in Islamic Theology.** 1965

Izutsu, Toshihiko. **God and Man in the Koran.** 1964

Jeffery, Arthur. **The Qur'ān as Scripture.** 1952

Jeffery, Arthur, editor. **A Reader on Islam.** 1962

Kritzeck, James and R. Bayly Winder, editors. **The World of Islam.** 1959

Muhammad 'Abduh. **The Theology of Unity.** 1966

Suhrawardy, Allama Sir Abdullah al-Mamun al-. **The Sayings of Muhammad.** 1941

Taftazani, Mas'ud ibn 'Umar al-. **A Commentary on the Creed of Islam.** 1950

Trimingham, J. Spencer. **Islam in East Africa.** 1964

Tritton, A.S. **Islam: Belief and Practices.** 1951